Cross-Cultural Leadership Studies

Cross-Cultural Leadership Studies

Alan S. Gutterman

BEP BUSINESS EXPERT PRESS

Cross-Cultural Leadership Studies

First published in 2019 by
Business Expert Press, LLC
222 East 46th Street, New York, NY 10017
www.businessexpertpress.com

ISBN-13: 978-1-94999-138-3 (paperback)
ISBN-13: 978-1-94999-139-0 (e-book)

Business Expert Press Human Resource Management and Organizational Behavior Collection

Collection ISSN: 1946-5637 (print)
Collection ISSN: 1946-5645 (electronic)

Cover and interior design by Exeter Premedia Services Private Ltd., Chennai, India

First edition: 2019

10 9 8 7 6 5 4 3 2 1

Printed in the United States of America.

Abstract

Leadership is a universal phenomenon that has preoccupied scholars, politicians, and others for centuries. In the management context leadership has been consistently identified as playing a critical role in the success or failure of organizations and some surveys have pegged almost half of an organization's performance on the quality and effectiveness of its leadership team. During the early years of serious research in the leadership area the focus was primarily on Western leadership styles and practices—not surprising given that U.S. researchers dominated the field; however, several factors—globalization of the workforce, expansion of operations into numerous markets around the world, and exposure to increased global competition—have forced leadership scholars to incorporate culture into their research and theories since leaders of businesses of all sizes in all countries must be prepared to interact with customers and other business partners from different cultures and leaders of larger companies have the additional challenge of managing multinational organizations and aligning a global corporate culture with multiple and diverging national cultures.

This book begins with an overview of the history and evolution of leadership studies that traces some of the major "schools" of leadership studies that have attracted the interest of researchers since the 19th century and discusses the various theories and models of leadership that have emerged over that period. The book then continues on to introduce cross-cultural leadership studies and the often intense debate among leadership scholars as to whether attributes of leadership are perceived in the same way—positively or negatively—across all societal cultures (i.e., universally), or whether the perception of those attributes varied across the range of societal cultures ("culturally contingent"). The book also discusses cross-cultural competencies of global leaders—the practical applications of the information available from the researchers to the day-to-day activities of leaders in business organizations around the world. Finally, the book assesses the research on cross-cultural leadership, reviews arguments that attempts by U.S. managers and consultants to transfer their theories of leadership to other countries will produce disappointing results due to the failure to understand cultural differences in the transferee countries, and discusses research on culture and leadership in developing countries.

Keywords

leadership; cross-cultural leadership; leadership theories; comparative leadership; cultural contingency; leadership in developing countries

Contents

Preface

The ongoing and extensive studies of leadership and the ways in which leaders and their subordinates, often referred to as "followers," have led to the advancement of a number of theories and models. For example, "trait" and "behavior" theories emphasize the personal characteristics of the leader. The leader's use of power and position to influence the actions of his or her followers is the focus of "power and influence" theory. Researchers using "contingency" and "contextual" theories are primarily interested in studying how the effectiveness of leader behaviors is impacted by the situation and characteristics of the subordinates. The nature and quality of the relationship between the leader and his or her subordinates is paramount in "transactional" theories and the attributions and perceptions of members of a society regarding leadership and the appropriate actions of leaders are the basis for "attributional" theories. Finally, "neocharismatic" or "transformational" theories of leadership are based on the premise that leaders can achieve extraordinary results through their use of "symbolic, emotional and highly motivating behaviors that appeal both to followers' minds and hearts."[1]

During the early years of serious research in the leadership area the focus was primarily on Western leadership styles and practices—not surprising given that U.S. researchers dominated the field; however, several factors—globalization of the workforce, expansion of operations into numerous markets around the world, and exposure to increased global competition—have forced leadership scholars to incorporate culture into their research and theories since leaders of businesses of all sizes in all countries must be prepared to interact with customers and other business partners from different cultures and leaders of larger companies have the additional challenge of managing multinational organizations

---

[1] Zagoršek, H. September 2004. "Assessing the Impact of National Culture on Leadership: A Six Nation Study." https://researchgate.net/publication/320274490_Leadership_A_Global_Survey_of_Theory_and_Research

and aligning a global corporate culture with multiple and diverging national cultures.

It has also been suggested that culture plays an important role in many aspects of how leaders develop and implement their leadership styles and how they interact with those persons who look to them for guidance. Early cross-cultural research regarding leadership focused on how cultural values impacted the authority of the leader, the personal characteristics of the leader (e.g., the leader's image in the eyes of his or her followers), the interpersonal actions between leaders and their followers, and the relationship between leaders and various groups within their organizations. For example, the applicable cultural values regarding power distance appeared to clearly have an impact on how leaders and their followers viewed the authority that the leader was entitled and expected to exercise—in large power distance societies it was presumed that leaders would have a substantial amount of authority that could and would be exercised with little in the way of input from followers regarding possible solutions and strategies. In addition, cultural preferences regarding "ideal" leadership styles and attributes that were articulated by followers could serve as the basis for the image that a leader attempted to craft in order to appear to be effective in that role.[2]

Following an important preliminary discussion of the history and evolution of leadership studies, this book continues with an introduction to cross-cultural leadership studies and the often intense debate among leadership scholars as to whether attributes of leadership are perceived in the same way—positively or negatively—across all societal cultures (i.e., universally), or whether the perception of those attributes varied across the range of societal cultures ("culturally contingent"). The book then continues with discussion, analysis, and criticism of the Global

---

[2] Dickson, M.W., D.N. Den Hartog, and J.K. Mitchelson. 2003. "Research on Leadership in a Cross-Cultural Context: Making Progress, and Raising New Questions." *The Leadership Quarterly* 14, no. 6, pp. 729–68, 760 (citing the discussion of a "culture enveloping model of leadership" described in Dorfman, P.W. 2003. "International and Cross-Cultural Leadership Research." In *Handbook for International Management Research*, eds. B. Punnett and O. Shenkar, 2nd ed. Ann Arbor, MI: University of Michigan).

Leadership and Organizational Behavior Effectiveness project, commonly referred to as "GLOBE," which was an ambitious effort to identify and measure relationships between culture and preferred leadership styles and behaviors. The GLOBE project was launched in large part to address an issue that was becoming increasingly clear—that theories of leadership needed to be revisited and, if necessary, updated to take into account the impact that culture has on how leadership is enacted in various societies around the world. Ardichvili and Kuchinke noted that in the mid-1990s scholars such as House had observed that the then-prevailing theories of leadership were dominated by North American characteristics with the result being that those theories were grounded in fundamental assumptions such as "individualism as opposed to collectivism, rationality rather than ascetics, hedonistic rather than altruistic motivation, centrality of work, and democratic value orientation."[3] As the decade ended, however, the evidence from research conducted in the areas of cross-cultural psychology and sociology was overwhelming that many cultures do not share those same assumptions and that it was likely that "characteristic leadership attributes" would vary across societies due to cultural differences.[4]

The book also discusses cross-cultural competencies of global leaders—the practical applications of the information available from the

---

[3] Ardichvili, A., and K. Kuchinke. 2002. "Leadership Styles and Cultural Values Among Managers and Subordinates: A Comparative Study of Four Countries of the Former Soviet Union, Germany and the US." *Human Resource Development International* 5, no. 1, pp. 99–117, 102. (referencing House, R.J. 1995. "Leadership in 21st Century: A Speculative Inquiry." In *The Changing Nature of Work*, eds. A. Howard. San Francisco: Jossey-Bass). Among the "prevailing" North American theories referred to in the quote were McGregor's Theory X and Theory Y, Likert's "System Four" management model and Blake and Mouton's "Managerial Grid."

[4] Den Hartog, D.N., R.J. House, P. Hanges et al. 1999. "Culture Specific and Cross-Culturally Generalizable Implicit Leadership Theories: are Attributes of Charismatic/Transformational Leadership Universally Endorsed?" *Leadership Quarterly* 10, no. 2, pp. 219–56. See also House, R.J. 1995. "Leadership in 21st Century: A Speculative Inquiry." In *The Changing Nature of Work*, 443. ed. A. Howard. San Francisco: Jossey-Bass, ("...there is a growing awareness of the need for a better understanding of the way that leadership is enacted in various cultures").

studies of the GLOBE researchers and others to the day-to-day activities of leaders in business organizations around the world. Finally, the book assesses the research on cross-cultural leadership, reviews earlier arguments of Hofstede that attempts by U.S. managers and consultants to transfer their theories of leadership to other countries will produce disappointing results due to the failure to understand cultural differences in the transferee countries, and discusses research on culture and leadership in developing countries.

CHAPTER 1

History and Evolution of Leadership Studies

Introduction

The time span of interest in "leadership" has been aptly summarized by Bass, who observed that

> ...[t]he study of leadership rivals in age the emergence of civilization, which shaped its leaders as much as it shaped them. From its infancy, the study of history has been the study of leaders—what they did and why they did it.[1]

In general, leadership studies have taken on a multidisciplinary flavor and one can find elements of theory and methodology borrowed from the social sciences, philosophy, psychology, and business administration. Leadership and management studies have often been combined and were originally studied and taught within schools of administration at universities and colleges; however, the recent trend is for leadership to be presented as a separate and distinguishable subject by schools that now specialize in business. That said, it is not practical to completely separate leadership and management studies given that it is widely acknowledged that "leading" is one of the functional managerial activities along with planning, organizing, and controlling. As leadership studies have evolved debates have constantly festered regarding definitions and scope of leadership and how to measure leadership effectiveness and declare leader actions to be "successful."

---

[1] Bass, B.M., and R.M. Stogdill's. 1990. *Bass & Stogdill's Handbook of Leadership: Theory, Research, and Managerial Applications*, 3. New York, NY: Free Press.

The sections that follow present brief descriptions of some of the major "schools" of leadership studies that have attracted the interest of researchers since the 19th century (see also Table 1.1). As with any scholarly

Table 1.1 *Major Schools of Leadership Studies*

Major Schools of Leadership Studies
Trait school of leadership: Sometimes referred to as the "great man" theory, this theory assumed that certain individual characteristics, or "traits," could be found in leaders but not in non-leaders and that those characteristics could not be developed but must be inherited (i.e., "great men were born, not made").
Behavioral school of leadership: Proponents of the behavioral school focused on the behaviors employed by leaders and the influence those behaviors had on the actions of their followers. In this instance, "behavior" referred to the how the leader treated his or her followers and how the leader viewed the role of the followers. Well-known, and contrasting, dimensions of leadership behavior included "employee-oriented" and "production-oriented" leadership.
Contingency school of leadership: Contingency theories were based on the premise that the effectiveness of leader behaviors in motivating their followers turned on various contingencies such as leader-member relations, the task structure, employee skills and experience, available information, the structure of the problem, and the support afforded the leader from superiors and the overall organization. Leaders were expected to adopt one of several different leadership styles (e.g., directive, supportive, participative, or achievement-oriented) based on the specific scenario confronting them.
Relational school of leadership: The best-known example of work under the umbrella of this school is the "leader-member exchange" theory, sometimes referred to as "LMX" theory or "transactional leadership," which attempted to describe the nature of the relationship between leaders and their followers and suggested two main alternatives: "high-quality" relations between a leader and his or her followers that were based on trust and mutual respect, referred to as the "in-group," and "low-quality" relations between a leader and followers based primarily on the satisfaction of contractual obligations, referred to as the "out-group."
Information processing school of leadership: This school focused on attempting to understand how and why the actions, behaviors, and styles of a leader might be "legitimized," and the leader accorded influence, because his or her personal characteristics (i.e., personality traits) match the prototypical expectations of followers with respect to their leaders.
"New leadership" (transformational) school: This school, variously referred to as "transformational," "charismatic," and "visionary," was characterized by the leader's use of various motivational practices that include inspiring followers to pursue and achieve a higher collective purpose, offering challenges, encouraging individual development, and creating a common mission and vision.

> **Contextual school of leadership:** This school is related to the contingency school discussed earlier and suggests that contextual, or situational, factors such as leader hierarchical level, national culture, leader-follower gender, and organizational characteristics give rise to or inhibit certain leadership behaviors or their dispositional antecedents.

Source: Descriptions based on Day, D., and J. Antonakis. 2012. "Leadership: Past, Present and Future." In *The Nature of Leadership*, eds D. Day and J. Antonakis, 3–25, 6–14, 2nd ed. Thousand Oaks, CA: Sage Publications.

discipline there is a lack of consensus regarding how research approaches should be categorized and, as noted as follows, the situation is becoming more complex as scholars begin to integrate pieces of different schools to create new models that are intended to be more comprehensive and provide new and different insights on questions of leadership. The following sections generally follow the classifications and ordering suggested by Day and Antonakis[2]; however, it should be noted that others have constructed slightly different lists and/or placed the work of certain researchers into different schools. For example, some lists might segregate research focusing on leadership skills and/or styles (e.g., participative versus autocratic leadership styles). Another common approach is to recognize a "situational" leadership approach that includes models developed by researchers such as Hersey and Blanchard, Vroom and Yetton, and House (i.e., the "path-goal" theory of leadership) that have been placed into different schools by Day and Antonakis.[3] Finally, the "leader-member exchange" theory discussed as the "relational school of leadership" in following is sometimes referred to as "transactional leadership."

Trait School of Leadership

One of the earliest and most popular conceptions of leadership that flourished in the 19th and early 20th centuries has been referred to as the

---

[2] Day, D., and J. Antonakis. 2012. "Leadership: Past, Present and Future." In *The Nature of Leadership*, eds. D. Day and J. Antonakis, 3–25, 6–14, 2nd ed. Thousand Oaks, CA: Sage Publications.

[3] Recognition of both "contingency" and "situational" leadership schools or approaches sometimes causes confusion; an important underlying premise for both of them is arguably quite similar: the appropriate leadership approach, behavior, and style should be tailored to the specific "context" or "situation" in which the leader is operating.

"great man" theory. This theory assumed that certain individual characteristics, or "traits," could be found in leaders but not in non-leaders and that those characteristics could not be developed but must be inherited.[4] In other words, the theory assumed that "great men were born, not made." Eventually the "great man" theory was discredited in the face of a continuous stream of new theories that had as one of their core principles the democratization of leadership opportunities. Slater and Bennis explained that

> [t]he passing years have ... given the coup de grace to another force that has retarded democratization—the 'great man' who with brilliance and farsightedness could preside with dictatorial powers as the head of a growing organization."[5]

The "great man" theory did leave behind a keen interest in attempting to identify those individual traits that could be most tightly linked to leadership and laid the foundation for the "trait school of leadership," which held that the traits of leaders—assumed to include their capacities, motives, and patterns of behavior—were different from those of non-leaders. In contrast to the "great man" theory, trait theories did not particularly care whether the leadership traits were inherited or acquired and, in fact, early suggestions about optimal traits included items that were inherited (e.g., height, weight, and physique) as well as items that were dependent on experience and training (e.g., industry knowledge).[6]

---

[4] Kirkpatrick, S.A., and E.A. Locke. 1991. "Leadership: Do Traits Matter?" *Academy of Management Executive* 5, no. 2, pp. 48–60, 48. For an interesting exploration of the "great man" theory, including exhaustive citations, see Eckmann, H. 2018. "Great Man Theory: A Personal Account of Attraction." Paper for the IBA Conference, http://jameslconsulting.com/documents/GreatManTheory.pdf (accessed December 31, 2018).

[5] Slater, P., and W.G. Bennis. September-October 1990. "Democracy is Inevitable." *Harvard Business Review* 68, no. 5, pp. 167–76, pp. 170–71.

[6] Kirkpatrick, S.A., and Locke, E.A. 1991. "Leadership: Do Traits Matter?" *Academy of Management Executive* 5, no. 2, pp. 48–60, 48. Kirkpatrick and Locke suggested that further information on trait theories and particular traits could be obtained by a review of Stogdill, R.M. 1974. *Handbook of Leadership: A Survey of Theory and Research.* New York, NY: Free Press; Boyatzis, R.E. 1982. *The*

Two of the most significant reviews of the trait school of leadership are attributed to Stodgill[7] and Mann[8] and there is evidence to support the proposition that certain traits, such as intelligence and dominance, are associated with leadership. However, many leadership scholars lacked confidence in the research findings relating to leadership traits. Stodgill himself wrote that "[a] person does not become a leader by virtue of the possession of some combination of traits."[9] Stodgill could find no support in the research for the presence of a group of traits that were universally associated with effective leadership and observed that situation factors played an important role in identifying the preferred strategies and behaviors for leaders. Kirkpatrick and Locke acknowledged that trait theories were largely abandoned for a significant period of time; however, they noted that new research using a variety of methods had provided support for the general proposition that effective and successful leaders were "different" and that there were a handful of core traits that were extremely important contributors to, albeit not guarantors of, the success of leaders in the business world.[10] They cautioned, however, that

> [t]raits alone…are not sufficient for successful business leadership—they are only a precondition" and that aspiring leaders with those traits must take certain actions in order to be successful such as formulating a vision, role modeling, and setting goals.[11] Antonakis et al. subsequently commented that, as of the

---

Competent Manager: A Model for Effective Performance. New York, NY: Wiley & Sons; Cox, C.J., and Cooper, C.L. 1988. *High Flyers: An Anatomy of Managerial Success*. Oxford: Basil Blackwell: and Yukl, G. 1989. *Leadership in Organizations*. Englewood Cliffs, NJ: Prentice Hall.

[7] Stodgill, R.M. 1948. "Personal Factors Associated with Leadership: A Survey of the Literature." *The Journal of Psychology* 25, no. 1, pp. 35–71.

[8] Mann, R.D. 1959. "A Review of the Relationships Between Personality and Performance in Small Groups." *Psychological Bulletin* 56, no. 4, p. 241.

[9] Stodgill, R.M. 1948. "Personal Factors Associated with Leadership: A Survey of the Literature." *Journal of Psychology* 25, no. 1, pp. 35–71, p. 64.

[10] Kirkpatick, S.A., and E.A. Locke. 1991. "Leadership: Do Traits Matter?" *Academy of Management Executive* 5, no. 2, pp. 48–60, 49.

[11] Id.

beginning of the 21st century, "the trait perspective appears to be enjoying a resurgence of interest.[12]

However, there has been a decline in the proportional interest in trait theories among published articles relating to leadership studies topics. Future areas of interest with respect to the study of traits include the impact of gender and other forms of "diversity."[13] In addition, researchers have explored measurement of directly observable individual differences (i.e., traits) from a new and novel biological or evolutionary perspective.[14]

Behavioral School of Leadership

The behavioral school of leadership became popular in the 1940s and 1950s as concerns began to emerge regarding the utility of focusing on

---

[12] Antonakis, J., A.T. Cianciolo, and R.J. Sternberg. 2004. "Leadership: Past, Present and Future." In *The Nature of Leadership*, eds. J. Antonakis, A. Cianciolo and R. Sternberg, 3–15, 7. Thousand Oaks, CA: Sage Publications,), Like Kirkpatrick and Locke, Antonakis et al. made note of research breakthroughs and referenced several studies that reinvigorated interest in identifying and proving links between leader characteristics and leader emergence including the work of scholars able to use new and more sophisticated analytical tools to "reanalyze" data compiled by earlier researchers. See, e.g., Lord, R.G., C.L. De Vader, and G.M. Alliger. 1986. "A Meta-Analysis of the Relation Between Personality Traits and Leadership Perceptions: An Application of Validity Generalization Procedures." *Journal of Applied Psychology* 71, no. 3, pp. 402–410 (reanalysis of data originally collected by Mann found a strong correlation between intelligence and leadership).

[13] Day, D.V., and J. Antonakis. 2012. "Leadership: Past, Present and Future." In *The Nature of Leadership*, eds. D.V. Day and J. Antonakis, 3–25, 8, 2nd ed. Thousand Oaks, CA: Sage Publications. For a recent review of the trait perspective on leadership, see Zaccaro, S.J. 2007. "Trait-Based Perspectives of Leadership." *American Psychologist* 62, no. 1, pp. 6–16.

[14] For a brief introduction to the "biological and evolutionary" perspectives, including citations, see Day, D.V., and J. Antonakis. 2012. "Leadership: Past, Present and Future." In *The Nature of Leadership*, D.V. Day and J. Antonakis, 3–25, 12, 2nd ed. Thousand Oaks, CA: Sage Publications. Areas being researched include the behavioral genetics of leadership emergence to leadership role occupancy. Id. (including citations). Another good introduction and overview can be found in Boyatzis, R. January 2011 "Nueroscience and Leadership." *Ivey Business Journal*.

leader traits. Proponents of the behavioral school focused their research activities on the behaviors employed by leaders and the influence those behaviors had on the actions of their followers. In this instance, "behavior" referred to the how the leader treated his or her followers and how the leader viewed the role of the followers in the grander organizational picture. During the 1950s two large studies were conducted by researchers at the University of Michigan[15] and the Ohio State University[16] and they identified two contrasting dimensions of leadership behavior: "consideration," often referred to as "employee-oriented" leadership, and "initiating structure," often referred to as "production-oriented" leadership. Similar research continued by Blake and Mouton[17] and others; however, findings were often contradictory and by the 1960s the general view was that success of leadership behaviors depended heavily on the "context" or "situation," thereby opening the door for the emergence of the "contextual" school of leadership referred to in the following. Antonakis et al. observed that while interest in behavioral theories has waned many of the ideas associated with the school have been incorporated into other theories, such as the contingency and transformational movements.[18]

Contingency School of Leadership

Contingency theories were based on the premise that the effectiveness of leader behaviors in motivating their followers turned on various

---

[15] Katz, D., N. Maccoby, G. Gurin, and L.G. Floor. 1951. *Productivity, Supervision and Morale Among Railroad Workers.*

[16] Stogdill, R.M., and A.E. Coons. 1957. *Leader Behavior: Its Description and Measurement.*

[17] Blake, R.R., and J. Mouton. 1964. *The Managerial Grid.* Houston, TX: Gulf. Their "leadership grid" included leadership styles that took into account both concern for production and concern for people. While they considered participatory, or team, management to be ideal, they realized that it might not be the most workable strategy in certain situations.

[18] Antonakis, J., A.T Cianciolo, and R.J. Sternberg. 2004. "Leadership: Past, Present and Future." In *The Nature of Leadership*, eds. J. Antonakis, A.T. Cianciolo and R.J. Sternberg, 3–15, 7. Thousand Oaks, CA: Sage Publications. (citing Lowe, K.B., and W.L. Gardner. 2000. "Ten Years of the Leadership Quarterly: Contributions and Challenges for the Future." *The Leadership Quarterly* 11, no. 4, pp. 459–514).

contingencies. For example, Fiedler argued that the choice of the most effective leadership behavior needed to take into account factors such as leader-member relations (i.e., the level of confidence that followers have in the skills and judgment of the leader and the intensity of follower attraction and loyalty toward the leader), the task structure (i.e., routine vs nonroutine), and the position of the leader (i.e., formal authority, including the ability to dispense rewards and punishments, and the support afforded the leader from superiors and the overall organization).[19] Another model generally assigned to the contingency school is House's "path-goal" theory, which focuses on ways that leadership behavior can motivate followers by clarifying the paths that they should take to achieve their goals and removing barriers to their performance.[20] House identified four possible leadership styles—directive, supportive, participative, and achievement-oriented—and argued that the success of these styles depended on employee contingencies (e.g., employee skills and experience) and environmental contingencies (e.g., task structure and team dynamics). One can see from the array of leadership styles championed by House that he believed that it was important for leaders to motivate and empower followers and enhance their self-confidence with respect to their ability to achieve their goals and perform at the highest level. The Vroom and Yetton model also identified different leadership styles based on the extent to which subordinates are allowed to participate in making decisions and suggested that contextual factors should determine which style is most appropriate and most likely to be effective. Their model suggested a series of questions that leaders can use to understand the context confronting them, including inquiries into quality and commitment requirements, whether the leader has sufficient information to make decisions on his or her own, the structure of the problem, commitment probability, goal congruence, subordinate conflict, and subordinate

---

[19] See Fiedler, F. 1967. *A Theory of Leadership Effectiveness*. New York, NY: McGraw-Hill. and Fiedler, F. 1971. *Leadership*. Morristown, NJ: General Learning.

[20] House, R. 1971. "A Path-Goal Theory of Leader Effectiveness." *Administrative Science Quarterly* 16, pp. 321–38.

information.[21] The contingency school remains relevant although the intensity of research has cooled since its heyday in the 1970s and 1980s.

Relational School of Leadership

The relational perspective school of leadership followed the contingency school and generated a fair amount of interest among researchers. Perhaps the best-known example of work under the umbrella of this school is the "leader-member exchange" theory, sometimes referred to as "LMX" theory, which attempts to describe the nature of the relationship between leaders and their followers and suggests two main alternatives: "high-quality" relations between a leader and his or her followers that are based on trust and mutual respect, referred to as the "in-group," and "low-quality" relations between a leader and followers based primarily on the satisfaction of contractual obligations, referred to as the "out-group." Not surprisingly, the LMX theory predicts that high-quality relations will lead to more effective and positive leader outcomes than low-quality relations.[22]

Skeptics of Leadership School

The so-called "skeptics of leadership" school combines a variety of criticisms of the efficacy and utility of leadership research raised during the

---

[21] Vroom, V., and P. Yetton. 1973. *Leadership and Decision Making*. Pittsburgh, PA: University of Pittsburgh Press. An expanded version of their model is common referred to as the "Vroom, Yetton, Jago Model". See Vroom, V.H., and A.G. Jago. 1988. *The New Leadership: Managing Participation in Organizations*. Englewood Cliffs, NJ: Prentice Hall.

[22] For discussion of LMX theory and empirical evidence regarding same, see Ilies, R., J. Nahrgang, and F. Morgeson. 2007. "Leader-Member Exchange and Citizenship Behaviors: A Meta-Analysis." *Journal of Applied Psychology* 92, pp. 269–277; Gerstner, C.R., and D.V. Day. 1997. "Meta-Analytic Review of Leader–Member Exchange Theory: Correlates and Construct Issues." *Journal of Applied Psychology* 82, no. 6, pp. 827–44; and Graen, G., and M. Uhl-Bien. 1995. "Relationship-Based Approach to Leadership: Development of Leader-Member Exchange (LMX) Theory of Leadership over 25 Years: Applying a Multi-level Multi-Domain Perspective." *The Leadership Quarterly* 6, no. 2, pp. 219–47.

1970s and 1980s.[23] For example, several researchers criticized ratings of leadership generated through the use of questionnaires lacked validity because they were "tainted" by the "implicit leadership theories" of those providing the ratings. In other words, the ratings reflected the implicit leadership theories that persons carry "in their heads" and that the actual behaviors and actions of the leaders themselves were irrelevant.[24] Another set of researchers also argued that leader behaviors and actions did not matter because followers actually based their assessments of their leaders primarily on the "outcomes" or results of the activities being led (i.e., the performance of the group that the leader is overseeing). These researchers argued that evaluations of the leader were simply part of the larger effort of followers "to understand and assign causes to organizational outcomes."[25] Meindl and Ehrlich and Pferrer even went so far as to question whether leadership existed or needed and expressed skepticism about whether leadership had any significant impact on the performance of organizations.[26] While interest in the work of the skeptics eventually waned in the face of counter-arguments by many other scholars who might aptly

---

[23] Antonakis, J., A.T. Cianciolo, and R.J. Sternberg. 2004. "Leadership: Past, Present and Future." In *The Nature of Leadership*, eds. J. Antonakis, A. Cianciolo and R. Sternberg, 3–15, 8. Thousand Oaks, CA: Sage Publications.

[24] See, e.g., Eden, D., and U. Leviathan. 1975. "Implicit Leadership Theory as a Determinant of the Factor Structure Underlying Supervisory Behavior Scales." *Journal of Applied Psychology* 60, no. 6, pp. 736–41; and Rush, M.C., J.C. Thomas, and R.G. Lord. 1977. "Implicit Leadership Theory: A Potential Threat to the Internal Validity of Leader Behavior Questionnaires." *Organizational Behavior and Human Performance* 20, no. 1, pp. 756–65.

[25] Antonakis, J., A.T. Cianciolo, and R.J. Sternberg. 2004. "Leadership: Past, Present, and Future." *The Nature of Leadership*, pp. 3–15. (citing Lord, R., J. Binning, M. Rush, and J. Thomas. 1978. "The Effect of Performance Cues and Leader Behavior on Questionnaire Ratings of Leadership Behavior." *Organizational Behavior and Human Performance* 21, no. 1, pp. 27–39).

[26] See Meindl, J.R., and S. Ehrlich. 1987. "The Romance of Leadership and the Evaluation of Organizational Performance." *Academy of Management Journal* 30, no. 1, pp. 90–109; and Pfeffer, J. 1977. "The Ambiguity of Leadership." *Academy of Management Review* 2, no. 1, pp. 104–12.

be referred to as "realists" rather than "skeptics,"[27] Antonakis et al. noted that this school improved the study of leadership in several ways, such as driving scholars to create and apply more rigorous research methodologies, differentiate top-level leadership from supervisory leadership, and focus on followers and how they actually perceive reality.[28]

Information Processing School of Leadership

The work of Lord et al. served as the foundation for what became known as the "information processing" school of leadership and focused on attempting to understand how and why the actions, behaviors, and styles of a leader might be "legitimized," and the leader accorded influence, because his or her personal characteristics (i.e., personality traits) match the prototypical expectations of followers with respect to their leaders.[29] The research in this area examined the steps taken by leaders in making decisions and the cognitive processes of followers as they gauged whether to accept the decisions of their leaders as legitimate and worth accepting and following. According to Antonakis et al. the information-processing approach has been extended and linked to other areas of leadership study and continues to generate interest within the research community.[30]

---

[27] See, e.g., Barrick, M.R., D.V. Day, R.G. Lord, and R.A. Alexander. 1991. "Assessing the Utility of Executive Leadership." *The Leadership Quarterly* 2, no. 1, pp. 9–22.

[28] Antonakis, J., A.T. Cianciolo, and R. Sternberg. 2004. "Leadership: Past, Present and Future." In *The Nature of Leadership*, eds. J. Antonakis, A. Cianciolo and R. Sternberg, 3–15, 9. Thousand Oaks, CA: Sage Publications.

[29] See, e.g., Lord, R.G., R.J. Foti, and C.L. De Vader. 1984. "A Test of Leadership Categorization Theory: Internal Structure, Information Processing, and Leadership Perceptions." *Organizational Behavior and Human Performance* 34, no. 3, pp. 343–78; Lord, R.G., and K.J. Maher. 1994. *Leadership and Information Processing: Linking Perceptions and Performance (People and Organizations)*. London: Routledge.

[30] Antonakis, J., A. Cianciolo, and R.J. Sternberg. 2004. "Leadership: Past, Present and Future." In *The Nature of Leadership*, eds. J. Antonakis, A. Cianciolo and R. Sternberg, 3–15, 9. Thousand Oaks, CA: Sage Publications.

"New Leadership" (Transformational) School

An exciting new paradigm of leadership, variously referred to as "transformational," "charismatic," and "visionary," took hold during the 1980s based primarily on the work of Bass and his associates,[31] who themselves built on earlier ideas developed by House[32] and Burns,[33] and others such as Bennis and Nanus.[34] Transformational leadership has been referred to as "a set of behaviors that transform followers' commitment and energy beyond the minimum levels prescribed by the organization."[35] Bass has written that transformational leaders influence their subordinates in three significant ways: (1) increasing their awareness of the importance of their tasks and the need to perform those tasks well; (2) making them aware of their own needs for personal growth, development, and accomplishment; and (3) motivating them to strive for the "good of the whole" as opposed to simply pursuing their own personal agendas.[36]

Transformational leadership has had a substantial impact on research and publication activities with respect to leadership studies over the last

---

[31] See, e.g., Bass, B.M. 1985. *Leadership and Performance Beyond Expectations.* New York, NY: Free Press; Bass, B.M. 1998. *Transformational Leadership: Industrial, Military, and Educational Impact.* Mahwah, NJ: Lawrence Erlbaum; and Bass, B.M., and B.J. Avolio. 1994. *Transformational Leadership: Improving Organizational Effectiveness.* Thousand Oaks, CA: Sage.

[32] House, R.J. 1977."A 1976 Theory of Charismatic Leadership." In *Leadership: The Cutting Edge,* eds. J. Hunt and L. Larson, 189–207. Carbondale, IL: Southern Illinois University Press.

[33] Burns, J.M. 1978. *Leadership.* New York, NY: Harper & Row.

[34] Bennis, W., and B. Nanus, *Leaders: The Strategies for Taking Charge* (New York: HarperCollins, 1985).

[35] Muczyk, J., and D. Holt. May 2008. "Toward a Cultural Contingency Model of Leadership." *Journal of Leadership & Organizational Studies* 14, no. 4, pp. 277–86, p. 280. (citing Podsakoff, P.M., S. MacKenzie, R. Moorman, and R. Fetter. 1990. "Transformational Leader Behaviors and their Effects on Followers' Trust in Leader, Satisfaction, and Organizational Citizenship Behaviors." *Leadership Quarterly* 1, no. 2, pp. 107–42).

[36] Muczyk, J., and T. Adler. 2002. "An Attempt at a Consentience Regarding Formal Leadership." *Journal of Leadership and Organizational Studies* 9, no. 2, pp. 2–17. (citing Bass, B.M. 1985. *Leadership and Performance Beyond Expectations.* New York, NY: Free Press).

two decades.[37] The proponents of the study of transformational leadership believed that much of the prior work with respect to leadership was "transactionally-oriented" and based on the fundamental premise that the relationship between leaders and followers was based on mutual satisfaction of transactional obligations. Bass, in particular, felt that this approach was incomplete and that a different form of leadership needed to be recognized "to account for follower outcomes centered on a sense of purpose and an idealized vision."[38]

Transformational leadership is characterized by the leader's use of various motivational practices that include inspiring followers to pursue and achieve a higher collective purpose, offering challenges, encouraging individual development, and creating a common mission and vision. According to Antonakis et al., the ideal of a transformational, or charismatic, leader was someone who could employ visionary and inspirational behaviors to motivate and inspire his or her followers to transcend their individual interests for the greater good of the entire organization.[39] Some of the "behaviors" commonly associated with transformational leadership include "individualized consideration," "intellectual stimulation,"

---

[37] The Bass model remains the predominant focus of research with respect to transformational leadership and Gardner et al. observed that all of the various models falling under the heading of "neo-charismatic" have been the most dominant paradigm in terms of publication activity in the leadership field over the first decade of the 21st century, although interest in relation to other areas declined from the prior decade due to renewed exploration of older topics such as "context" and "traits" and the rise of new topics such as leadership development. See Gardner, W.L., K.B. Lowe, T.W. Moss, K.T. Mahoney, and C. Cogliser. 2010. "Scholarly Leadership of the Study of Leadership: A Review of the Leadership Quarterly's Second Decade, 2000–2009." *The Leadership Quarterly* 21, no. 6, pp. 922–58.

[38] Antonakis, J., A.T. Cianciolo, and R. Sternberg. 2004. "Leadership: Past, Present and Future." In *The Nature of Leadership*, eds. J. Antonakis, A. Cianciolo and R. Sternberg, 3–15, 9. Thousand Oaks, CA: Sage Publications. See also Bass, B.M. 1996. *A New Paradigm of Leadership: An Inquiry into Transformational Leadership*. Alexandria, VA: Army Research Institute for the Behavioral and Social Sciences. (reviewing a series of studies that support the distinction between transformational and transactional leadership).

[39] Id. at 9–10.

"charisma," and "inspirational motivation."[40] Lists of characteristics or traits of transformational leaders include identification of self as a change agent, courage, belief in people, being value-driven, lifelong learner, ability to deal with complexity, and "visionary."[41]

Lowe et al., among others, have evaluated transformational leadership and declared it to be effective and positively related to subordinate satisfaction, motivation, and performance.[42] A number of studies have found a high degree of correlation among the four transformational leadership styles, which suggests that transformational leadership behaviors typically occur in clusters (i.e., a leader who is perceived by his or her followers as charismatic is also likely to be perceived as motivating and concerned about the individual needs of his or her followers).[43] While it is generally acknowledged that transformational leadership can be a relevant and valuable principle for actions of leaders at the top of the organizational hierarchy as they set the strategy course for the entire organization, other types of leadership practiced at lower levels of the hierarchy, including transactional leadership, remain important. In addition, Bass often claimed that transformational leadership was endorsed in many cultural

---

[40] Ardichvili, A., and K.P. Kuchinke. 2002. "Leadership Styles and Cultural Values Among Managers and Subordinates: A Comparative Study of Four Countries of the Former Soviet Union, Germany and the US." *Human Resource Development International* 5, no. 1, pp. 99–117, p. 101 (citing Bass, B.M. 1985. *Leadership and Performance beyond Expectations*. New York, NY: The Free Press.) The behaviors associated with transformational leadership are measured with the Multifactor Leadership Questionnaire. See Avolio, B.J., B.M. Bass, and D. Jung. 1995. *MLQ: Multifactor Leadership Questionnaire: Technical Report*. Palo Alto, CA: Mind Garden.

[41] Tichy, N., and M. Devanna. 1986. *The Transformational Leader*. New York, NY: John Wiley & Sons.

[42] Lowe, K.B., K. Kroeck, and N. Sivasubramaniam. 1996. "Effectiveness Correlates of Transformational and Transactional Leadership: A Meta-Analytic Review of the MLQ Literature." *Leadership Quarterly* 7, pp. 385–425.

[43] Ardichvili, A., and K.P. Kuchinke. 2002. "Leadership Styles and Cultural Values Among Managers and Subordinates: A Comparative Study of Four Countries of the Former Soviet Union, Germany and the US." *Human Resource Development International* 5, no. 1, pp. 99–117, 110.

contexts and thus had "universal" applicability and utility,[44] and the findings of the researchers involved in the Global Leadership and Organizational Behavior Effectiveness ("GLOBE") project and others appear to indicate that culture does impact both the enactment and effectiveness of transformational leadership techniques and that aspects of both transformational and transactional leadership can coexist in certain societies concurrently.[45]

Muczyk and Adler emphasized that the traditional notion of "transformational leadership" assumed that leaders were able to influence their subordinates "through inspiration created by the interaction of vision and charisma and enable by position power."[46] They noted that "vision" could be distinguished from the formal, long-term strategic plan that is

---

[44] Bass, B.M. 1997. "Does the Transactional-Transformational Leadership Paradigm Transcend Organizational and National Boundaries?" *American Psychologist* 52, no. 2, pp. 130–39; and Bass, B.M., and B. Avolio. 1989. *Manual: The Multifactor Leadership Questionnaire.* Palo Alto, CA: Consulting Psychologists Press. Other works cited for the proposition that it was unlikely that transformational leadership varied significantly from culture to culture include Koene, H., H. Pennings, and M. Schreuder. 1993. "Leadership, Culture, and Organizational Effectiveness." In *The Impact of Leadership*, eds. K. Clark and M. Clark. Greensboro, NC: Center for Creative Leadership; Koh, W.L., R.M. Steers, and J.R. Terborg. 1995. "The Effects of Transformational Leadership on Teacher Attitudes and Student Performance in Singapore." *Journal of Organizational Behavior* 16, no. 4, pp. 319–34; House, R.J., A. Hanges, P. Ruiz-Quintanilla, M. Dorfman, and M. Dickson. 1998. "Cultural Influences on Leadership and Organizations: Project GLOBE." In *Advances in Global Leadership*, ed. W. Mobbley Greenwich, CT: JAI; Javidan, M., and D. Carl. 1997. "Motivational Consequences of Charismatic Leadership: An Empirical Investigation." Working Paper, School of Business Administration, University of Calgary; and Pereira, D. 1987. "Factors Associated with Transformational Leadership in an Indian Engineering Firm." Paper presented at Administrative Science Association of Canada, Vancouver.

[45] See, e.g., Ardichvili, A., and K.P. Kuchinke, "Leadership Styles and Cultural Values Among Managers and Subordinates: A Comparative Study of Four Countries of the Former Soviet Union, Germany and the US." *Human Resource Development International* 5, no. 1, pp. 99–117.

[46] Muczyk, J.P., and T. Adler. 2002. "An Attempt at a Consentience Regarding Formal Leadership." *Journal of Leadership and Organizational Studies* 9, no. 2, pp. 2–17.

developed through the assessment of organizational strengths and weaknesses and opportunities and threats in the organizational environment. In fact, Campbell and Alexander defined "vision" in this context as "an inspired, long-run strategy that is not obvious to managers and executives until it is revealed by the transformational leader."[47] Certainly there are many who would confirm the proposition that "vision is the essence of leadership"; however, a number of leaders dismiss the notion as little more than some "esoteric thing no one can quantify" and argue that while there is no doubt that leaders must have a "sense of the future, if not an inspired vision, to prosper" they are better served by aligning their core competencies with opportunities through sound business planning and then pursuing success through deft execution.[48] Still another attribute not mentioned in the connection with "transformational leadership" that Collins found to be among the common characteristics of leaders who moved their companies from "good" to "great" was "perseverance," including the discipline and tenacity to follow a strategy through once it was selected and overcome difficult tasks and situations that might arise along the road.[49]

Muczyk and Adler also challenged both the importance of "charisma" and the suggestion that charismatic individuals could only be found at the top of the organizational hierarchy in the personality of the man or woman placed in the highest leadership position.[50] Muczyk and Adler observed that it was probably fair to say that "charismatic leaders are

---

[47] Id. (citing Campbell, A., and M. Alexander. November-December 1997. "What's Wrong with Strategy?" *Harvard Business Review*, pp. 42–51).

[48] Id. See also Lavin, D. October 4, 1993. "Robert Eaton Thinks Vision Is Overrated And He's Not Alone." *The Wall Street Journal*, A1 (quoting Bill Gates of Microsoft as saying "Being a visionary is trivial").

[49] Muczyk, J.P., and T. Adler. 2002. "An Attempt at a Consentience Regarding Formal Leadership." *Journal of Leadership and Organizational Studies* 9, no. 2, pp. 2–17. (citing Collins, J. 2001. *Good to Great*. New York, NY: Harper Business).

[50] Kirkpatrick and Locke questioned the importance of "charisma" for business leaders and suggested that perhaps it may only be important for political leaders. Kirkpatrick, S.A., and E.A. Locke. 1991. "Leadership: Do Traits Matter?" *Academy of Management Executive* 5, no. 2, pp. 48–60, 56.

born rather than made" and that this limited the pool of candidates for traditional "transformational leadership"; however, as was the case when they discussed how vision had little value without effective execution, Muczyk and Adler pointed out that many of the fundamental processes of management, the "blocking and tackling" to use a football metaphor, did not require "charisma," including "redefining the role and size of staff departments, de-layering hierarchies, continually improving processes and practices through re-engineering, employing network organizations where appropriate, empowering employees, establishing a strong connection between performance and rewards, and placing customers first."[51]

Muczyk and Adler did not go so far as to say that "transformational leadership" did not exist or wasn't necessary; they simply observed that in their opinion transformational leadership was needed only at the top of the organization and only in those organizations that fit a particular profile, including a crisis situation that required "dramatic" acts. In addition, they felt that leadership of some sort came from those persons who might be disqualified from "transformational leader" status due to a lack of "charisma." All in all, Muczyk and Adler sounded a cautionary tale about the need to rush to find a "transformational leader" to dramatically and mysteriously pull organizations out of their malaise overnight. In addition to their skepticism regarding the importance of "vision" and "charisma" and their criticism of the apparent lack of recognition given to "execution," Muczyk and Adler argued that "the preponderance of successful leaders build incrementally over time rather than transforming organizations overnight."[52] In fact, they urged that organizations should be less concerned about finding a "transformational leader" and pay more attention to avoiding what they referred to as a "dysfunctional leader" who throws an organization that is already in trouble into turmoil and chaos ("regressive transformation" in their words) through the selection and use of ineffective leadership techniques.

---

[51] Muczyk, J.P., and T. Adler, "An Attempt at a Consentience Regarding Formal Leadership." *Journal of Leadership and Organizational Studies* 9, no. 2, pp. 2–17.
[52] Id. Muczyk and Adler also cited a quote from Robert Earon, who served as CEO of Chrysler: "I believe in quantifiable short-term results—things we can all relate to—as opposed to some esoteric thing [vision] no one can quantify."

Critique and Assessment of Established Leadership Studies Traditions

It is common to present the various schools, or traditions, of leadership studies in chronological order, as has been done earlier, to provide a sense of the evolution of research and theory in this area. However, Zaccaro and Klimoski have provided an alternative perspective for surveying and critiquing the established leadership studies traditions by suggesting that they can be segregated into four categories: social and interpersonal exchange, strategic management, organizational systems theory, and performance effectiveness models of leadership.[53] Their description and assessment of each of these categories are described in more detail in the following sections. In general, their view is that each of these traditions has provided specific insights for understanding various aspects of leadership but that each of them has certain limitations that ultimately led them to suggest their own model that is based on understanding the "performance imperatives" confronting the senior leaders of an organization.

Social and Interpersonal Exchange

Zaccaro and Klimoski observed that the social exchange approach to leadership was probably the most popular and pervasive perspective in the literature.[54] This approach focused primarily on the leader-follower relationship and the underlying theme of most of the theories associated with this approach was described as follows: "leaders provide direction, guidance, and activity structuring to the collective; members of the collective in turn grant the leader permission to influence them (therefore conferring legitimacy), as well as reverence and respect."[55] Leadership effectiveness turns on the quality of the dynamic that exists between leader and followers.

---

[53] Zaccaro, S.J., and R. Klimoski. 2001. "The Nature of Organizational Leadership: An Introduction." In *The Nature of Organizational Leadership* (*Understanding the Performance Imperatives Confronting Today's Leaders*), eds. S. Zaccaro and R. Klimoski, 1–41, 14–26. New York, NY: John Wiley & Sons.

[54] Id. at 14.

[55] Id.

Zaccaro and Klimoski argued that models from this approach focused on or more of three elements: leader characteristics, follower characteristics, and/or relationship characteristics. Researchers interested in leader characteristics generally focus on the styles used by the leader to interact with his or her followers, with the primary distinction being made between task- and relationship-orientation. Well-known examples of these types of models include Likert's "System Four" management model and Blake and Mouton's "Managerial Grid," each of which are discussed elsewhere in this Guide.[56] Researchers proposing theories based on follower characteristics studied the processes that followers use to grant "legitimacy" status to leaders, including the development of "implicit" leadership theories,[57] and often use this information to provide guid-

---

[56] Likert, R. 1961. *New Patterns of Management*. New York, NY: McGraw-Hill. and Blake, R.R., and Mouton, J.S. 1964. *The Managerial Grid*. Houston: Gulf. Zaccaro and Klimoski provides citations to a number of other examples of models based on distinctions between task- and relationship orientation including Fleishman, E.A. 1953. "The Description of Supervisory Behavior." *Personnel Psychology* 37, no. 1, pp. 1–6, and Fleishman, E.A. 1973. "Twenty Years of Consideration and Structure." In *Current Developments in the Study of Leadership*, eds. E. Fleishman and J. Hunt, Carbondale, IL: Southern Illinois University Press. (defining initiating structure and consideration as the two key and contrasting leadership behaviors); Fiedler, F.E. 1964. "A Contingency Model of Leadership Effectiveness." In *Advances in Experimental Social Psychology*, ed. L. Berkowitz, 1 Vol. Orlando, FL: Academic Press, and Fiedler, F.E. 1971. "Validation and Extension of the Contingency Model of Leadership Effectiveness: A Review of the Empirical Findings." *Psychological Bulletin* 76, no. 2, pp. 128–48. (contingency model using task- versus group-oriented dimensions); and Hersey, P., and K.H. Blanchard. 1969. *Management of Organizational Behavior: Utilizing Human Resources*. Upper Saddle River, NJ: Prentice Hall.

[57] See, e.g., Hollander, E.P. 1958. "Conformity, Status, and Idiosyncrasy Credit." *Psychological Review* 65, no. 2, pp. 117–27; Hollander, E. 1979. "Leadership and Social Exchange Processes." In *Social Exchange: Advances in Theory and Research*, eds. K. Gergen, M. Greenberg and R. Willis, New York, NY: Winston/Wiley; Hollander, E.P., and J.W. Julian. 1970. "Studies in Leader Legitimacy, Influence, and Motivation." In *Advances in Experimental Social Psychology*, ed. L. Berkowitz, 5 vol. Orlando, FL: Academic Press; and Cronshaw, S., and R. Lord. 1987. "Effects of Categorization, Attribution, and Encoding Processes on Leadership Perceptions." *Journal of Applied Psychology* 72, no. 1, pp. 97–106.

ance to prospective leaders on the behavioral styles they should adopt in order to influence their followers. Finally, researchers concentrating on leader-follower relationships have investigated the overall quality of the relationship, the degree to which the leader and followers are mutually influential (e.g., is the relationship "participative," meaning influence flows both ways, or "directive/autocratic," meaning influence flows only from the leader), and the degree to which followers feel empowered (e.g., transformational leadership).[58]

Zaccaro and Klimoski acknowledged that the various models associated with the social exchange approach have made extensive and valuable contributions to leadership studies, including enhanced understanding of key issues such as what constitutes an effective exchange between leaders and subordinates, how leader qualities and behaviors facilitate subordinate and small group effectiveness, how the contributions of various leadership styles to subordinate effectiveness are moderated by a variety of situational factors, and how the characteristics and information processing

---

[58] Zaccaro, S., and R. Klimoski. 2001. "The Nature of Organizational Leadership: An Introduction." In *The Nature of Organizational Leadership* (Understanding the Performance Imperatives Confronting Today's Leaders), S. Zaccaro and R. Klimoski, 1–41, 15. New York, NY: John Wiley & Sons. (citing, e.g., with respect to overall quality of the leader-subordinate relationship, Fiedler, F.E. 1964. "A Contingency Model of Leadership Effectiveness." In *Advances in Experimental Social Psychology*, ed. L. Berkowitz, 1 Vol. Orlando, FL: Academic Press. and Fiedler, F.E. 1971. "Validation and Extension of the Contingency Model of Leadership Effectiveness: A Review of the Empirical Findings." *Psychological Bulletin* 76, no. 2, pp. 128–48; with respect to mutuality of influence, Vroom, V.H., and A. Jago. 1974. "Decision Making as a Social Process: Normative and Descriptive Models of Leader Behavior." *Decision Sciences* 5, pp. 743–69, Vroom, V.H., and A.G. Jago. 1978. "On the Validity of the Vroom-Yetton Model." *Journal of Applied Psychology* 63, no. 2, pp. 151–62 and Vroom, V.H., and A.G. Jago. 1995. "Situation Effects and Levels of Analysis in the Study of Leader Participation." *Leadership Quarterly* 6, no. 2, pp. 169–81; and, with respect to transformational leadership, Bass, B.M. 1985. *Leadership and Performance Beyond Expectations*. New York, NY: Free Press; Bass, B.M. 1996. *A New Paradigm of Leadership: An Inquiry into Transformational Leadership*. Alexandria, VA: U.S. Army Research Institute for the Behavioral and Social Sciences.

of subordinates contribute to effective leadership.[59] However, they also argued that this approach had several crucial shortcomings that limited their ability to provide a full understanding of organizational leadership. For example, Zaccaro and Klimoski felt that since social exchange models focused primarily on direct interactions between leaders and followers they were best suited to the study of individual, small group, and direct leadership and failed to provide a solid basis for understanding leadership in situations where leaders rarely have face-to-face interactions with their followers (i.e., executive leadership). In other words, social exchange theories are more suited for lower-level leadership than executive leadership. Zaccaro and Klimoski also noted that social exchange theories failed to give due weight and consideration to importance leadership processes such as information acquisition, sense making and giving, and long-range strategic decision making.

Strategic Management

Zaccaro and Klimoski referred to models of strategic decision making as those models and theories that focus primarily on the strategic decision-making activities of the top executives, or leaders, of the organization.[60] The underlying premise for these models is that organizational effectiveness depends on the ability of senior organizational leaders to create and manage tight alignment between the organization and its environment. Zaccaro and Klimoski noted that researchers interested in the strategic management approach have focused on leadership processes such as environmental scanning, sense making and giving, specification of strategic choices, and selection and implementation of appropriate strategies.[61] Other variations of the strategic management approach include models focusing on the fit between organizational strategy and

---

[59] Zaccaro, S.J. and R.J. Klimoski. 2001. "The Nature of Organizational Leadership: An Introduction" In *The Nature of Organizational Leadership* (*Understanding the Performance Imperatives Confronting Today's Leaders*), eds. S. Zaccaro and R. Klimoski, 1–41, 16. New York, NY: John Wiley & Sons.

[60] Id. at 17.

[61] Id.

the personal characteristics of its top managers, with strategy being a determinant rather than a consequence of executive selection and strategy,[62] and models focusing on the thought processes and characteristics of top leaders as they process information and use it in order to make strategic decisions.[63] A relatively recent development has been increased interest in the dynamics of the strategic decision-making process among the members of the top management team.[64]

As might be expected after the discussion of social exchange approaches as shown earlier, Zaccaro and Klimoski praised the strategic decision-making theories for their contributions in increasing understanding of important aspects of executive leadership, particularly the cognitive and planning processes employed by executives.[65] Zaccaro and Klimoski also recognized the emphasis that strategic decision-making theories placed on contextual factors such as environmental and organizational forces. In short, these theories were seen as extremely useful in understanding "large-scale" leadership (i.e., leadership of large organizations). However,

---

[62] The major research figure with respect to this model is Anil Gupta and reference should be made to Gupta, A.K. 1984. "Contingency Linkages Between Strategy and General Managerial Characteristics: A Conceptual Examination." *Academy of Management Review* 9, no. 3, pp. 399–412, and Gupta, A.K. 1988. "Contingency Perspectives on Strategic Leadership: Current Knowledge and Future Research Directions." In *The executive Effect: Concepts and Methods for Studying Top Managers*, ed. D. Hambrick. Greenwich, CT: JAI Press.

[63] See, e.g., Bourgeois, III, L.J. 1985. "Strategic Management and Determinism." *Academy of Management Review* 9, no. 4, pp. 586–96; and Bourgeois, III, L.J. 1985. "Strategic Goals, Perceived Uncertainty, and Economic Performance in Volatile Environments." *Academy of Management Journal* 28, no. 3, pp. 548–73.

[64] See, e.g., Amason, A.C. 1996. "Distinguishing the Effects of Functional and Dysfunctional Conflict on Strategic Decision Making: Resolving a Paradox for Top Management Teams." *Academy of Management Journal* 39, no. 1, pp. 123–48, and Hambrick, D.C. 1994. "Top Management Groups: A Conceptual Integration and Reconsideration of the "Team" Label." In *Research in Organizational Behavior*, 16 Vol. Greenwich, CT: JAI Press.

[65] Zaccaro, S.J., and R.J. Klimoski. 2001. "The Nature of Organizational Leadership: An Introduction" In *The Nature of Organizational Leadership* (Understanding the Performance Imperatives Confronting Today's Leaders), eds. S. Zaccaro and R. Klimoski, 1–41, 19. New York, NY: John Wiley & Sons.

Zaccaro and Klimoski concluded that strategic decision-making theories are limited by their relative neglect of "direct interpersonal processes" that are prominent features of the social exchange approaches and also important to truly understanding how strategies are selected, communicated, and implemented.[66]

Organizational Systems

Zaccaro and Klimoski referred to models of the organizational systems approach as those that "emphasize the boundary spanning and internal coordination responsibilities of leaders within open social systems."[67] Systems theory has been applied in a number of disciplines; however, Katz and Kahn are probably the most well-known proponents of viewing organizations as "open systems in close transactional relationship with their resource-providing environments."[68] A simplistic description of the Katz and Kahn model includes five key concepts: inputs, throughput, output, systems as cycles of events, and negative feedback. Organizations convert inputs of energy and information from their external environment into outputs that can be exported back out to the external environment using a set of interlocking throughput activities. The inputs of energy may include people, materials, or resources from other organizations and informational inputs include signals from the external environment including negative feedback. Throughput activities include all the actions and decisions necessary to reorganize the inputs to transform them into the products or services that the organization seeks to reintroduce into the external environment (i.e., market and sell to customers). Since the entire process is seen as a system the process of exchanging and transforming energy must renew the system and thus create a stream of continuous activities. As this process continues the system should collect and analyze internal information about the operational functioning of the system so that corrections can be made with respect to energy intake and production

---

[66] Id.

[67] Id.

[68] Id.

processes so that the organization can remain on track in relation to its performance indicators.[69]

Zaccaro and Klimoski noted that the throughput process in the Katz and Kahn model is extremely important and complex and is generally accomplished through the creation of "connected subsystems" within the organization such as subsystems primarily responsible for actions and resources such as production, procurement, and personnel (i.e., human resources). When organizations are viewed as open systems it is clear that "[a]n essential function of management is to coordinate the activities of integrated units."[70] This function, which also includes maintaining interconnectedness within the system, applies to every manager, regardless of where they might be in the organizational hierarchy; however, the challenges become more difficult for leaders near the top of the hierarchy since they must deal with interactions among a large number of units engaged in a diverse range of activities. In addition, the impact of changes in the external environment must also be taken into account and Zaccaro and Klimoski argue that another major responsibility of organizational leaders is monitoring the external environments of their organizational units and identifying and promoting changes in the system thought to be necessary in order to cope with critical changes in those environments. Again, environmental monitoring and adaptive response to changes should be a priority for all organizational leaders at every level although obviously a first-line supervisor will have a much narrower "external environment" than a CEO who needs to monitor the environment for the entire organization and deal with a much higher level of complexity and lack of structure.[71] Zaccaro and Klimoski noted that top executives not only need to "span the boundary between the entire organization and more complex and unstructured environment" but are also responsible for coordinating the activities of their own "system" with other organizations that have

---

[69] Id. at 19–20. For full description of the Katz and Kahn model, see Katz, D., and R.L. Kahn. 1978. *The Social Psychology of Organizations*, 2nd ed. New York, NY: Wiley.

[70] Id. at 20.

[71] Id. at 20–21.

become linked to that system through partnering arrangements.[72] This sort of activity not only includes oversight of key strategic alliances but also participation in lobbying efforts with competitors in order to obtain advantages for all industry participants.

Zaccaro and Klimoski provided the following description of Zaccaro's conclusions regarding the organizational systems perspective based on an extensive review of the executive leadership literature[73]:

- Leader performance requirements can be described in terms of three distinct levels in organizational space.
- All organizational leaders engage in direction setting (such as goal setting, planning, strategy making, and envisioning) for their constituent units. Such direction setting incorporates an increasingly longer time frame at higher organizational levels.
- All organizational leaders engage in boundary-spanning activities, linking their constituent units with their environments. At lower organizational levels, this environment is the broader organization. At upper levels, boundary spanning and environmental analysis occur increasingly within the organization's external environment.
- All organizational leaders are responsible for operational maintenance and coordination within the organization. At upper levels, operational influence becomes increasingly indirect.
- The effective accomplishment of executive performance functions facilitates organizational performance and success.
- Characteristics of the operating environment influence the nature and quality of executive performance requirements.

---

[72] Id.

[73] Id. at 21 (quoted verbatim). The conclusions described in the text originally appeared in Zaccaro, S.J. 1996. *Models and Theories of Executive Leadership: A Conceptual/Empirical Review and Integration.* Alexandria, VA: U.S. Army Research Institute for the Behavioral and Social Sciences.

Zaccaro and Klimoski viewed the organizational systems approach as a significant contribution to the understanding of organizational leadership and were particularly impressed by the organization-wide perspective and recognition of how the roles and activities of leaders change as one goes up and down the organizational hierarchy. They were, however, critical of the failure of models in this approach to adequately take into account the performance imperatives in the leader's operating environment that influence his or her activities. In addition, they commented that the organizational systems approach failed to give enough attention to "the links among leader attributes, the leadership functions articulated by systems models and organizational effectiveness."[74]

Other researchers have studied and analyzed organizations as open systems that "have the ability to self-organize if the proper context is preserved."[75] Viewed in this fashion, organizations do not exist in isolation but rather share a semi-permeable boundary with their external environment. As a result, the organization effectively merges with its environment and there is a constant flow of information going back and forth between the organization and its environment that affects and enhances the organization and influences the way the organization is structured and operates. Fairholm referred to this process as "autopoiesis"—a process whereby a system produces its own organization and maintains and constitutes itself in a space—and argued that recognition of the process created an imperative for organizational leaders to adopt the following leadership practices and approaches to maintain their organizations as identifiable entities in a turbulent environment while at the same time leading those organizations through the changes and adaptions necessary to cope with continuing environmental challenges[76]:

- Allow and encourage the free flow of information from and to all levels of the organization's hierarchy, thereby supporting the development of a sense of community that promotes trust

---

[74] Id. at 22.

[75] Fairholm, M.R. 2004. "A New Sciences Outline for Leadership Development." The Leadership and Organization Development Journal 25, no. 4, p. 369.

[76] Id. at 371–374.

and individual autonomy. Fairholm was critical of previous prescriptions to leaders to buffer and filter information
received from internal and external environments.

- Ensure that continuous feedback loops are forged and
maintained throughout the organization to achieve the best
advantage from creativity, the internal organizational culture, and external flows of information. Credible reliance
on, and support of, feedback loops is also a sign of a leader's
self-confidence.

- Maintain a relationship focus that recognizes that people are
the fundamental parts of the organization and that relationships among people are the "essential building blocks of a
flexible and sustainable organization." Building strong relationships within the organization is essential for ensuring the
strength and integrity of the channels through which information will flow throughout the organization.

- Build a "trust culture" in which both the leader and his or
her followers can comfortably and reliably trust the purposes,
actions, and intentions of others and work together to further
the goals of the organization based on shared values.

Leader Effectiveness

While not without opposition, the general assumption among students
of leadership studies is that "leadership matters" and does have an impact
on organizational effectiveness and the leader effectiveness approach
includes those models and theories of organizational leadership that focus
on identifying and explaining "connections between leader attributes and
organizational effectiveness."[77] The historical foundation for leadership
effectiveness theories is the trait school of leadership described previously
and while interest in the study of leader traits and attributes has ebbed

---

[77] Zaccaro, S.J., and R.J. Klimoski. 2001. "The Nature of Organizational Leadership: An Introduction." In *The Nature of Organizational Leadership* (*Understanding the Performance Imperatives Confronting Today's Leaders*), eds. S. Zaccaro and
R. Klimoski, 1–41, 23. New York, NY: John Wiley & Sons.

and flowed over the years there is clearly renewed focus on identifying those personal attributes of leaders that can be tied through empirical evidence to organizational success. Zaccaro and Klimoski noted that the leadership effectiveness approach and search for essential personal attributes have contributed to "a focus on leader assessment, selection, training, and development systems that enhance these attributes" and that research efforts had been made to validate the connections between particular leadership attributes and key leadership processes and organizational effectiveness.[78] They cited, for example, the efforts of the longitudinal assessment center research conducted at American Telephone and Telegraph ("ATT") and the studies relating to leadership development conducted by the Center for Creative Leadership ("CCL").[79] The ATT researchers found that characteristics such as "need for power," interpersonal and cognitive skills, and motivational orientations were significant predictors of career advancement. The CCL research found that managers with the following characteristics were more likely to fail once they had reached higher levels of management, even after succeeding at lower management levels: putting personal advancement ahead of personal integrity, weak interpersonal skills, and narrowly focused with respect to technical and cognitive skills. Nonetheless, Zaccaro and Klimoski concluded that additional work was still needed in order to achieve an appropriate level of understanding and also noted that more consideration needed to be given to the diversity of performance imperatives confronting organizational leaders.

Emerging Trends and Issues

While controversy has often existed, and still remains, within the field of leadership studies, it is generally agreed that a good deal of progress has been made and that a number of interesting paths for future research and

---

[78] Id.

[79] Id. at 24 (citing Bray, D., R. Campbell and D. Grant. 1974. *Formative Years in Business: A Long-term AT & T Study of Managerial Lives*. New York, NY: Wiley; and McCall, M., and M. Lombardo. 1983. *Off the Track: Why and How Successful Executives Get Derailed*. Greensboro, NC: Center for Creative Leadership).

understanding have been uncovered. In 2004 Antonakis et al. identified several areas that they believed warranted further research, including "context," ethics, and leadership traits.[80] Several years later Day and Antonakis updated the original list to add diversity issues relating to leadership as an important area for greater research emphasis.[81] Another promising trend is the efforts of many scholars to integrate various conceptualizations of leadership to consolidate existing knowledge and generate new theories and models with greater explanatory value. Ideas regarding leadership are also emerging from rapid and stunning discoveries in new sciences such as quantum physics, chaos theory, and complexity science that are being imported into the social sciences.

Context is the primary subject matter of the so-called "contextual school of leadership," which is related to the contingency school discussed earlier and suggests that "contextual factors ... give rise to or inhibit certain leadership behaviors or their dispositional antecedents."[82] Potential contextual factors include leader hierarchical level, national culture, leader-follower gender, and organizational characteristics.[83] Contextual, or situational, factors are central to pragmatic leadership prescriptions of Hersey and Blanchard, who created a three-dimensional model for

---

[80] Antonakis, J., A.T. Cianciolo, and R.J. Sternberg. 2004. "Leadership: Past, Present and Future." In *The Nature of Leadership*, eds. J. Antonakis, A. Cianciolo and R. Sternberg, 3–15, 10–11. Thousand Oaks, CA: Sage Publications.

[81] Day, D.V., and J. Antonakis. 2012. "Leadership: Past, Present and Future." In *The Nature of Leadership*, eds. D.V. Day and J. Antonakis, 3–25, 10–11, 2nd ed. Thousand Oaks, CA: Sage Publications.

[82] Id. at 10. For further information and evidence on the "contextual school of leadership", see Shamir, B., and J.M. Howell. 1999. "Organizational and Contextual Influences on the Emergence and Effectiveness of Charismatic Leadership." *The Leadership Quarterly* 10, no. 2, pp. 257–83; Hannah, S.T., M. Uhl-Bien, B.J. Avolio, and F.L. Cavaretta, "A Framework for Examining Leadership in Extreme Contexts." *The Leadership Quarterly* 20, no. 6, pp. 897–919; Porter, L.W., and G.B. McLaughlin. 2006. "Leadership and Organizational Context: Like the Weather?" *The Leadership Quarterly* 17, no. 6, pp. 559–76.

[83] Antonakis, J., B.J. Avolio, and N. Sivasubramaniam. 2003. "Context and Leadership: An Examination of the Nine-factor Full-Range Leadership Theory using the Multifactor Leadership Questionnaire." *The Leadership Quarterly* 14, no. 3, pp. 261–95.

achieving effective leadership based on the following principles: leaders exhibit both task and relationship behaviors, with task behaviors focusing on organization, definition, and direction of work activities and relationship behaviors focusing on providing support and encouragement to followers; leader effectiveness depends on the proper alignment of leadership style to the particular situation; and an important situational factor is the willingness and ability of followers to perform necessary tasks and activities.[84] Zaccaro and Klimoski urged for the study of leadership "in situ" and argued for particular attention to the dimensions of organizational structure such as hierarchical level and the degree of differentiation in function and to the specific cultural and societal parameters that the leader must deal with in his or her particular position.[85]

As for ethics, Day and Antonakis have commented that "the ethics of leadership and a leader's level of moral development are increasingly becoming essential elements of leadership research and theory."[86] Bass was one of the first to build ethics into a leadership model but did not do so until almost 10 years after his theory was first developed when he added the distinction between authentic (i.e., ethical) and inauthentic (i.e., unethical) transformational leaders.[87] Day and Antonakis have urged researchers to continue to build the ethics of leader means and outcomes

---

[84] See, e.g., Hersey, P., and K.H. Blanchard. January 1996. "Great Ideas: Revisiting the Life-Cycle Theory of Leadership." *Training and Development* 50, no. 1, pp. 42–47; and Hersey, P., and Blanchard, K.H. 1993. *Management of Organizational Behavior*. Englewood Cliffs, NJ: Prentice-Hall. The work of Hersey and Blanchard is often categorized under the umbrella of the so-called "situational school of leadership".

[85] Zaccaro, S.J., and R.J. Klimoski. 2001 "The Nature of Organizational Leadership: An Introduction." In *The Nature of Organizational Leadership* (*Understanding the Performance Imperatives Confronting Today's Leaders*) eds. S. Zaccaro and R. Klimoski, 1–41, 4. New York, NY: John Wiley & Sons.

[86] Day, D.V., and J. Antonakis. 2012. "Leadership: Past, Present and Future." In *The Nature of Leadership*, eds. D.V. Day and J. Antonakis. 2nd ed. 3–25, 13. Thousand Oaks, CA: Sage Publications. See also Brown, M.E., and L.K. Trevino. 2006. "Ethical Leadership: A Review and Future Directions." *The Leadership Quarterly* 17, no. 6, pp. 595–616.

[87] Bass, B.M., and P. Steidlemeier, "Ethics, Character, and Authentic Transformational Leadership Behavior." *The Leadership Quarterly* 10, no. 2, pp. 181–217.

into their leadership models and explore ways in which the ethical and moral orientations of leaders can be developed and otherwise improved.[88]

One of the most interesting areas for further research is the plethora of issues raised while exploring relationships between diversity and leadership. As time goes by the pool of leaders and followers worldwide has expanded beyond the traditional "white male" to include an extremely diverse group in terms of culture, gender, race and ethnicity, and sexual orientation.[89] Substantial advances have been made with respect to understanding and analyzing the relationship between leadership and societal culture and the impact of gender differences has also received more attention in the recent past.[90] Day and Antonakis noted that research relating to leadership and race and ethnicity and sexual orientation is still trailing; however, it is expected that these shortcomings will be addressed as part of a wave of exploration of leadership and diversity.[91]

As previously noted, interest in the study of leadership traits has experienced a resurgence due in part to progress that has been made defining alternative conceptions of various traits and in linking them

---

[88] For further information and discussion regarding ethics, morality and leadership, see Day, D.V., M. Harrison, and S. Halpin. 2009. *An Integrative Approach to Leader Development: Connecting Adult Development, Identity, and Expertise.* New York, NY: Routledge; and Turner, N., J. Barling, O. Epitropaki, V. Butcher, and C. Milner. "Transformational Leadership and Moral Reasoning." *Journal of Applied Psychology* 87, no. 2, pp. 304–11.

[89] Day, D.V., and J. Antonakis. 2012. "Leadership: Past, Present and Future." In *The Nature of Leadership*, eds. D.V. Day and J. Antonakis, 2nd ed. 3–25, 13. Thousand Oaks, CA: Sage Publications, For further discussion, see A.H. Eagly, and J.L. Chin. 2010. "Diversity and Leadership in a Changing World." *American Psychologist* 65, no. 3, pp. 216–24.

[90] With regard to leadership and societal culture, see House, R.J., P.J. Hanges, M. Javidan, P.W. Dorfman, and V. Gupta. 2004. *Culture, Leadership, and Organizations: The GLOBE Study of 62 Societies.* Thousand Oaks, CA: Sage. With regard to leadership and gender, see Eagly, A.H., and L.L. Carli. 2007. *Through the Labyrinth: The Truth about How Women Become Leaders.* Boston, MA: Harvard Business School Press.

[91] With regard to leadership and race, for example, see Livers, A., and K. Caver. 2003. *Leading in Black and White: Working Across the Racial Divide in Corporate America.* San Francisco: Jossey-Bass.

to leadership emergence/effectiveness. One example is the way that the trait of "cognitive ability," traditionally seen as a unitary concept largely related to academic ability, has been reconceptualized to acknowledge and measure other important factors such as a person's creative and problem-solving abilities.

Antonakis et al. also encouraged the development and testing of new leadership models that integrate some of the overlapping and comple-mentary conceptualizations of leadership that have been promoted over the years in order to create new hybrid theories and models of leader-ship.[92] One of the attempts to integrate overlapping perspectives of lead-ership that they noted was the framework of executive leadership created by Zaccaro that integrated elements of cognitive, behavioral, strategic, and visionary leadership theories.[93] Bass' integration of transformational and transactional leadership theories, which is discussed elsewhere in this Guide, is another illustration of how seemingly different pieces can be woven together to provide a richer explanation of what leadership is and how it works.

Another emerging trend in the study of leadership is the attempt to apply concepts derived from advances in the so-called "new sciences" (i.e., quantum physics, autopoietic theories found in biology, chaos theory, and complexity science) to develop reinterpretations of traditional leader-ship theories and practices.[94] Fairholm argued that four general principles taken from the new sciences provided a "new metaphor for organizational life and the work of leadership"[95]:

---

[92] Antonakis, J., A.T. Cianciolo, and R.J. Sternberg. 2004. "Leadership: Past, Present and Future." In *The Nature of Leadership*, eds. J. Antonakis, A. Cianciolo and R. Sternberg, 3–15, 11. Thousand Oaks, CA: Sage Publications. See also Avolio, B.J. 2007. "Promoting more Integrative Strategies for Leadership Theory Building." *American Psychologist* 62, no. 1, pp. 25–33.

[93] Zaccaro, S.J. 2001. *The Nature of Executive Leadership: A Conceptual and Empir-ical Analysis of Success.* Washington, DC: American Psychological Association.

[94] Fairholm, M.R. 2004. "A New Sciences Outline for Leadership Development." *The Leadership and Organization Development Journal* 25, no. 4, pp. 369–83. See also Margaret J. Wheatley. 2006. Leadership and the New Science: Discovering Order in a Chaotic World, 3rd ed. San Francisco: Berrett-Koehler Publishers.

[95] Id. at 372.

- Autopoiesis: Organizations, as "open systems," are able to self-organize if the proper context is preserved
- Paradox: Uncertainty and ambiguity are a part of organizational life
- Fields and attractors: Organizations and the people within them cluster around inherent structuring forces
- Fractals: Simple principles and patterns may create complex structures through random (noncontrolled), autonomous action

Fairholm went on to suggest various "leadership technologies" for coping with each of these general principles:

- Self-organization that leads to a harmonious workplace in which everyone is working together toward mutual objectives is a highly desirable outcome for an organizational leader that can be promoted by allowing information to flow freely, designing continuous feedback loops, maintaining a relationship focus, and instilling and encouraging trust.
- Uncertainty and ambiguity should be seen as opportunities for learning and beneficial change and leaders must make the effort to "get on the balcony" (i.e., remove themselves from day-to-day pressures in order to see the "big picture"), understand the creative destruction cycle and, most importantly, proactively lead followers through the necessary transitions.
- Visions and values serve as organizational attractors and attention should be paid to each of them as a means for setting and altering organizational culture. Leaders must develop a clear statement of values and emphasize those values at every opportunity. At the same time, leaders must listen to and watch the value of their followers. Values must then be translated into a dynamic and compelling vision for the organization by the leader and the leader must teach and coach followers to accept and apply the vision and the values that support that vision.

- Leaders must recognize that their role is more about shaping principles and patterns as opposed to exerting command and control over their followers and Fairholm argued that leaders should replace standard operating procedures and policy manuals with "short, simple statements reflecting the values and vision of the organization." These simple guidelines should be supplemented by encouragement of autonomous action, a recognition that qualitative aspects of the organization are most important than quantitative measures, and a willingness to delegate authority and foster the development and growth of followers into new leaders in their own right.

Fairholm observed that the above-described principles and technologies provided a means for designing training and development programs for leaders and argued that the theoretical framework derived from the lessons of the new sciences was more descriptive of organizational realities than previous models that assumed that all aspects of human life, including organizations, operated with mechanistic predictability. Training programs would need to focus on the various skills necessary for leaders to effectively and genuinely execute the suggested technologies. For example, development of relationships and comfort with delegation requires that leaders learn new ways to interact with followers and open their hearts and minds to equal and sharing communications with followers during which both sides exchange ideas and provide counsel and advice to the other. Fairholm referred to this as "counciling-with" others and pointed out that it was a shared approach commonly associated with the democratic and participative styles of leadership and management.[96]

---

[96] Id. at 380.

CHAPTER 2

Cross-Cultural Leadership Studies

Introduction

It is fair to say that a good deal of the activity with respect to cross-cultural studies over the past years has focused on cross-cultural leadership. Culture plays an important role in many aspects of how leaders develop and implement their leadership styles and how they interact with those persons who look to them for guidance. Dickson et al. have noted the growing acceptance of cross-cultural leadership as an identifiable and independent field of study and research separate from the most established and well-known fields of cross-cultural research and leadership research.[1] The research conducted regarding leadership has focused on how cultural values impact the authority of the leader, the personal characteristics of the leader (e.g., the leader's image in the eyes of his or her followers), the interpersonal actions between leaders and their followers, and the relationship between leaders and various groups within their organizations. For example, the applicable cultural values regarding power distance appear to clearly have an impact on how leaders and their followers view the authority that the leader is entitled and expected to exercise—in large power distance societies it is presumed that leaders will have a substantial amount of authority that can and will be exercised with little in the way of input from followers regarding possible solutions and strategies. In addition, cultural preferences regarding "ideal" leadership styles and attributes

---

[1] Dickson, M.W., D.N. Den Hartog, and J.K. Mitchelson. 2003. "Research on Leadership in a Cross-Cultural Context: Making Progress, and Raising New Questions." *The Leadership Quarterly* 14, no. 16, pp. 729–68, p. 748.

that are articulated by followers can serve as the basis for the image that a leader attempts to craft in order to appear to be effective in that role.[2]

Dickson et al. have cited several factors that have contributed to the emergence of cross-cultural leadership research including the proliferation of publication outlets for cross-cultural leadership research and the launch of several large studies of the relationship between leadership and culture (e.g., the Global Leadership and Organizational Behavior Effectiveness ("GLOBE") project) involving a number of countries and multiple investigators drawn from around the world with their own cultural backgrounds and the corresponding ability to bring a different viewpoint to the questions asked and the data that is collected.[3] These two factors are related to some extent because the growth of publication outlets has provided additional incentives for researchers, most of which come from the academic community, to embark on the larger, more time-intensive multinational studies. In addition, researchers looking to carve a niche

---

[2] Id. at 760 (citing the discussion of a "culture enveloping model of leadership" described in Dorfman, P.W. 2003. "International and Cross-Cultural Leadership Research." In *Handbook for International Management Research*, eds. B. Punnett and O. Shenkar, 2nd ed. Ann Arbor, MI: University of Michigan).

[3] Id. at 748. Dickson et al. referred to several examples of the publication outlets in this area including *The Leadership Quarterly*, the 2002 issue of *The Journal of World Business* focusing on the GLOBE project and a biennial series titled *Advances in Global Leadership* published by JAI Press. The researchers who launched *Advances in Global Research* provided a short, but useful, list of the potential advantages of comparative management studies and cross-cultural studies. First of all, they sought to facilitate understanding of the interplay between national and organizational cultures, organizational strategy, the stage of development of the organization and/or business units within the organization, as well understanding of individual differences. Second, they were interested in evaluating the generalizability of models and practices developed in Western cultures, particularly leadership and management practices used in the United States. Finally, research relating to multicultural and global leadership has expanded to address the challenges that managers now commonly confront when working in "nontraditional" organizational structures such as joint ventures and strategic alliances. See Mobley, W., and M. McCall., eds. 2001. *Advances in Global Leadership*, 2 Vol. New York, NY: JAI Press.

in the emerging field of cross-cultural leadership studies are anxious to contribute their talents to ambitious undertakings such as the GLOBE project, which has generated an extensive body of literature on numerous countries and so-called "outcomes of interest." Interest in multinational studies has also been enhanced by improvements in necessary technological and analytic tools that allow researchers from all parts of the world to communicate and collaborate and work effectively with large amount of data is well organized and adaptable for rigorous statistical analysis.

The large multinational studies have addressed several of the criticisms commonly made of traditional research in both comparative management studies and cross-cultural studies—the excessive reliance on two-culture studies that provide very limited information that is difficult to place within the broader context of the literature in the applicable discipline. For example, while it may be interesting to hear that a researcher claims to have discovered differences between a group of farmers in Country A and a group of farmers in Country B with respect to a commonly recognized cultural dimension such as uncertainty avoidance this information often creates more questions than answers including the following: has a similar study using the same variables and measures been done among farmers in two or more different countries, which would provide a broader context for the results of the Country A/Country B study; would the results of the Country A/Country B study be the same if different measures of chosen variables were used or the study was conducted by a researcher with a different cultural background; or would the results of the Country A/ Country B study be different if the sample groups consisted of lawyers (or some other group) instead of farmers. Carefully constructed multinational studies reduce a number of potential problems associated with studies of a small number of countries by introducing uniformity of the instruments and construct definitions used in data collection and analysis phases, tapping into the cultural diversity of investigative team members from around the world, not just one country such as the United States, and generating data from multiple cultures that can be subjected to sophisticated statistical analysis (i.e., multiple regression) to provide significantly greater insights into whether a particular cultural dimension influences an "outcome of interest" and, if so, just how strong that influence might be.[4]

GLOBE represents the largest and arguably most influential multinational study of national culture and the impact of culture on leadership styles and behaviors. While Hofstede and others may quarrel with the path that the GLOBE researchers took with regard to instrument design and data analysis it is nonetheless important to take note of some of the innovative techniques that GLOBE sought to introduce to the field. The GLOBE researchers themselves provided the following list of what they regarded as the strengths of their approach as part of their response to various criticisms of GLOBE lodged by Hofstede: theory-driven constructs; a total of over 160 researchers from 62 societies were involved in the research design from the very beginning and they conducted individual and focus group interviews with managers in their own countries; all of the local investigators received questionnaire items and provided reports on their face validity, understandability, and relevance in their own cultures; items were edited on the basis of these reports and new items were added; the final draft of the items went through a very rigorous psychometric process for instrument design; the surviving instruments were translated and back-translated in each country; pilot tests were conducted in several countries to empirically verify whether the cultural dimensions common source error was controlled for in the

---

[4] Dickson, M.W., D.N. Den Hartog, and J.K. Mitchelson. 2003. "Research on Leadership in a Cross-Cultural Context: Making Progress, and Raising New Questions." *The Leadership Quarterly* 14, no. 6, pp. 729–68, pp.748–49. A number of multinational studies have actually been launched to test for broader applicability of findings identified in earlier single country studies. For example, one study collected data from a number of countries with differing cultural dimensions to support the claims of Bass that transformational leadership is endorsed in a number of different cultures. See Ardichvili, A. 2001. "Leadership Styles and Work-Related Values of Managers and Employees of Manufacturing Enterprises in Post-Communist Countries." *Human Resource Development Quarterly* 12, no. 4, pp. 363–83. One of the criticisms of Bass had been that his claims were primarily based on results obtained in studies within a single country that compared transformational to transactional leadership styles in just one cultural context.

research design; rigorous statistical procedures to verify that the scales are aggregable, unidimensional, and reliable, and to ensure cross-cultural differences; state-of-the-art statistical techniques (HLM) were used to test a priori hypotheses, showing that the culture-to-leadership relationships existed at organizational or societal level, not individual level; rigorous statistical evidence for relationship between societal and organizational culture; and multimethod-multitrait analysis and multilevel confirmatory factor analysis to establish construct validity.[5]

Multinational studies have been used with respect to a number of issues other than those addressed by Hofstede and the GLOBE researchers to test the broader applicability of findings in earlier single-country studies. For example, Bass was a long-standing proponent of transformational leadership and often claimed that transformational leadership was endorsed in many cultural contexts.[6] Others took issue with Bass on the basis that his argument regarding the cross-cultural popularity of transformational versus transactional leadership was based primarily on one-country studies carried out in a single cultural context. Eventually, however, researchers such as Ardichvili collected data from multiple cultures that could be analyzed with respect to Bass' transformational-transactional leadership and other cultural dimensions.[7]

While the increase in the number and scope of multinational studies is encouraging and exciting there are still significant drawbacks with the approaches taken with respect to designing the studies and collecting and evaluating the data. As noted by Dickson et al.:

[5] Javidan, M., R.J. House, P.W. Dorfman, P.J. Hanges, and M.S. de Luque. 2006. "Conceptualizing and Measuring Cultures and their Consequences: A Comparative Review of GLOBE's and Hofstede's Approaches." *Journal of International Business Studies* 37, no. 6, pp. 897–914, 910.

[6] See, e.g., Bass, B.M. 1997. "Does the Transactional-Transformational Leadership Paradigm Transcend Organizational and National Boundaries?" *American Psychologist* 52, no. 2, pp. 130–39.

[7] See Ardichvili, A. 2001. "Leadership Styles and Work-Related Values of Managers and Employees of Manufacturing Enterprises in Post-Communist Countries." *Human Resource Development Quarterly* 12, no. 4, pp. 363–83.

Despite the substantial advances these studies represent, there are still significant limitations present in the majority of them. Most consider relatively few cultures or focus specifically on one region of the world. Some measure culture, others simply apply the culture dimension scores found by Hofstede or others. The measures of leadership also vary. Some focus on a specific behavior or aspect, some on ideologies or preferred leadership and some test models developed in one region of the world in another world region. Still others do not refer to leadership as such, but test attitudes and behaviors that are relevant to the understanding of leadership in different cultures. Many studies rely on surveys as their sole method.[8]

The new tools available to researchers in the cross-cultural leadership area have also allowed them to explore a number of interesting propositions and issues that have long fueled debate in the field. For example, in 1997 House et al. advanced several interesting propositions that they referred to as cultural congruence, cultural difference, and the near universality of leadership behaviors.[9] Each of these propositions, which are subsequently discussed in detail, have interesting and important consequences in relation to the way in which leaders behave and their expectations with regard to the actions of their followers in reaction to certain leadership behaviors. The GLOBE project explicitly explored the issue of universality of leadership behaviors; however, other studies have also contributed to the debate and it is reasonable to expect that the volume of research will continue to grow in the years to come particularly research on the specific role and impact of cultural differences on leadership styles and behaviors that appear to be culturally contingent. Other questions

---

[8] Dickson, M.W., D.N. Den Hartog, and J.K. Mitchelson. 2003. "Research on Leadership in a Cross-Cultural Context: Making Progress, and Raising New Questions." *The Leadership Quarterly* 14, no. 6, pp. 729–68, p. 751.

[9] House, R.J., P. Hanges, and S. Ruiz-Quintanilla. 1997. "GLOBE: The Global Leadership and Organizational Behavior Effectiveness Research Program." *Polish Psychological Bulletin* 28, no. 3, pp. 215–54.

that researchers have wrestled with include gauging the effect of "global-ization" on cultural differences and the rate of cultural change.

Cultural Congruence

The proposition of "cultural congruence" argued that the cultural values in the environment in which a leader is working will determine which lead-ership behaviors or attributes will be most effective in that environment.[10] Since it was first proposed a number of studies have been undertaken to provide evidence to support this proposition. For example, one study found that China's cultural values of conformity and tradition possi-bly explained why Chinese managers preferred management styles that avoided conflict while at the same time U.S. managers, operating under achievement-oriented cultural values, tended to use competing conflict management styles.[11] Another study provided support for the relationship between cultural values and the preferred level of subordinate involve-ment in decisions that managers are required to make regarding strategy and operations. Specifically, managers were more likely to tap into the experience of subordinates and allow them to participate in decisions when the societal cultural values included high individualism, cultural autonomy, egalitarianism, low power distance, harmony, and femininity; however, supervisorial authority and formal rules played much bigger roles in the making of decisions—and subordinate participation was min-imal or nonexistent—in societies characterized by collectivism, cultural embeddedness, hierarchy, power distance, mastery, and masculinity.[12]

---

[10] Id.

[11] Morris, M.W., K.Y. Williams, K. Leung, R. Larrick, M.T. Mendoza, D. Bhatmager, J.C. Hu. 1998. "Conflict Management Style: Accounting for Cross-National Differences." *Journal of International Business Studies* 29, no. 4, pp. 729–47.

[12] Smith, P.B., M.F. Peterson, and S.H. 2002. "Cultural Values, Sources of Guidance, and their Relevance to Managerial Behavior—A 47-Nation Study." *Journal of Cross-Cultural Psychology* 33, no. 2, pp. 188–208.

Cultural Difference Proposition

The cultural difference proposition laid out the interesting and intriguing idea that if leaders adopted behaviors and attributes that were slightly different than what was traditionally expected and accepted under the dominant cultural values of the society they would be able to encourage innovation and improvements in performance simply by introducing "change" provided that the disruption was not too radical.[13] This sort of "unconventional behavior" has been tied to the actions that leaders are encouraged to take to implement the charismatic leadership style.[14] However, there has not been much in the way of research evidence to support this proposition.

Universality Versus Cultural Contingency

Many researchers believe that the fundamental question in cross-cultural studies is identifying "emics" and "etics." In their words, "[e]mics are things that are unique to a culture, whereas etics are things that are universal to all cultures. Emics are by definition not comparable across cultures."[15] The foregoing explains why so much of the research done with respect to cross-cultural studies, particularly in the general area of "leadership," has focused on what things or phenomena are "universal" (i.e., etics) and what things or phenomena are "culturally contingent" (i.e., emics).[16] The quest for universality has been challenging for a number of

---

[13] House, R.J., P. Hanges, and S. Ruiz-Quintanilla. 1997. "GLOBE: The Global Leadership and Organizational Behavior Effectiveness Research Program." *Polish Psychological Bulletin* 28, no. 3, pp. 215–54.

[14] See, e.g., Conger, J.A., and R.N. Kanungo. 1987. "Toward a Behavioral Theory of Charismatic Leadership in Organizational Settings." *Academy of Management Review* 12, no. 4, pp. 637–47.

[15] Graen, G.B., C. Hui, M. Wakabayashi, and Z. Wang. 1997. "Cross-Cultural Research Alliances in Organizational Research." In *New Perspectives on International Industrial/Organizational Psychology, eds.* P. Earley and M. Erez, 160–89, 162. San Francisco, CA: Jossey-Bass.

[16] Dickson, M.W., P.J. Hanges, and R.G. Lord. 2001. "Trends, Developments, and Gaps in Cross-Cultural Research on Leadership." In *Advances in Global Leadership*, eds. W. Mobley and M. McCall, 2 vol. Stamford, CT: JAI Press.

reasons beginning with the fact that several different types of "universal relationships" have been identified in the literature[17]:

The simple universal is a thing or phenomenon that is constant throughout the world and can be generalized across cultural boundaries. For example, the general idea of "leadership" is a universal phenomenon since some form of leadership can be found in all societies and certain leadership behaviors—"encouraging," "positive," "motivational," "dynamic," and "excellence-oriented"—also appear to be viewed favorably in all countries included in large representative samples.[18]

The variform universal is a general statement or principle that applies across all cultures but that plays out differently from culture to culture (i.e., culture moderates the relationship). For example, "organizational citizenship" exists in some form in all cultures but its enactment plays out differently depending on the cultural context.[19]

The functional universal occurs when the "within-group" relationship between two variables is the same across cultures. For example, it has been suggested that the more that a leader engages in transformational behaviors the more effective he or she will be as a leader regardless of the cultural context and therefore leaders who develop a vision of the future

---

[17] Based on Dickson, M.W., D.N. Den Hartog, and J.K. Mitchelson. 2003. "Research on Leadership in a Cross-Cultural Context: Making Progress, and Raising New Questions." *The Leadership Quarterly* 14, no. 6, pp. 729–68, 732–33. The first three types were identified in Lonner, W.J. 1980. "The Search for Psychological Universals." In *Perspectives Handbook of Cross-Cultural Psychology*, eds. J. Triandis and W. Lambert, 1 vol. Boston: Allyn and Bacon, 1980. and the last two types were introduced in Bass, B.M. 1997. "Does the Transactional-Transformational Leadership Paradigm Transcend Organizational and National Boundaries?" *American Psychologist* 52, no. 2, pp. 130–39.

[18] The leadership behaviors referenced in the text are characteristic of "transformational leadership" and were analyzed in a large study on the effectiveness of transformational behavior that was part of the GLOBE research program.

[19] See Farh, J.L., P.C. Earley, and S. Lin. 1997. "Impetus for Action: A Cultural Analysis of Justice and Organizational Citizenship Behavior in Chinese Society." *Administrative Science Quarterly* 42, pp. 421–44 (describing how enactment of organizational citizenship is different in an Asian context).

and motivate their followers to work hard will be effective wherever they might be.[20]

The variform functional universal occurs when the relationship between two variables is found in every culture but the magnitude of the relationship between the variables is different from culture to culture. For example, researchers have examined the idea that while behaviors embodying transformational leadership are meaningful in all cultural contexts their enactment is demonstrably different depending on whether the context is Eastern or Western.[21]

The systematic behavioral universal is a theory that claims either (a) a sequence of behavior (i.e., "if-then") is invariant in all cultures or (b) the structure and organization of a behavior or behavioral cluster is constant in all cultures.

The pursuit of universality was common in many of the earliest research efforts in the field of cross-cultural studies; however, Hofstede, among others, eventually turned the discussion in a different direction

---

[20] Bass, B.M. 1997. "Does the Transactional-Transformational Leadership Paradigm Transcend Organizational and National Boundaries?" *American Psychologist* 52, no. 2, pp. 130–39 (citing research supporting the effectiveness of transformational leadership in India, Japan, New Zealand and Singapore). Another study of the impact of transformational leadership on teachers' commitment to change found similarities in North America and Hong Kong; however, the magnitude of the impact was much less among teachers in Hong Kong. See Yu, H., K. Leithwood, and D. Jantzi. 2002. "The Effects of Transformational Leadership on Teachers' Commitment to Change in Hong Kong." *Journal of Educational Administration* 40, nos. (4–5), pp. 368–90.

[21] See Spreitzer, G.M., K.H. Perttula, and K. Xin. 2018. "Traditionality Matters: An Examination of the Effectiveness of Transformational Leadership in the U.S. and Taiwan." http://webuser.bus.umich.edu/spreitze/traditionalitymatters.pdf (accessed December 31, 2018). See also Jung, D.I., B.M. Bass, and J.J. Sosik. 1995. "Bridging Leadership and Culture: A Theoretical Consideration of Transformational Leadership and Collectivist Cultures." *The Journal of Leadership Studies* 2, no. 4, pp. 3–18 (suggesting that transformational leadership is generalizable but that it is more important in societies that can be categorized as "collectivist" since followers in those societies are more comfortable with the recommended focus of transformational leaders on collective mission, goals and responsibilities).

through his efforts to demonstrate that "culture matters" when predicting the efficacy of leadership styles and management practices. Universality of leadership behaviors was of particular interest to the GLOBE researchers and House et al. laid out the "near universality of leadership behaviors proposition," which held that there are leadership attributes that are either universally accepted as effective or universally perceived as impediments to effective leadership, regardless of the cultural values of the specific society.[22] A number of studies, particularly the GLOBE project, focused on testing this proposition and results seemed to support the proposition although the research also confirmed that the effect of a much wider array of leadership attributes is culturally contingent.

Supporters of the cultural contingency approach argue that leadership theories that originate in the Anglo-American culture may not be universally applicable in countries with different cultural orientation because those theories are grounded in and defined by the Western values of the persons who came up with and popularized the theories. In fact, there is a good deal of research that supports cultural contingency in the area of leadership—persons with different cultural values do perceive and react to leadership styles and methods differently. For example, one group of researchers concluded that certain transformational leadership styles that are popular and appear to be successful in Western cultures would not be effective in Columbia, India, or the Middle East and that a leader in those countries would be better off deploying leadership behaviors that are directive and less involved with followers.[23] Differences in the effectiveness of leadership styles between cultures were also uncovered in a number of studies conducted as part of the GLOBE project. For example, Den Hartog et al. found universal endorsement of several attributes of charismatic/transformational leadership as being associated

---

[22] House, R.J., P. Hanges, and S. Ruiz-Quintanilla. 1997. "GLOBE: The Global Leadership and Organizational Behavior Effectiveness Research Program." *Polish Psychological Bulletin* 28, no. 3, pp. 215–54.

[23] Pillai, R., T.A. Scandura, and E. Williams. 1997. "Are there Universal Models of Leadership and Organizational Justice? An Investigation of the U.S., Australia, India, Columbia, and the Middle East." *Journal of International Business Studies* 30, pp. 763–79.

with outstanding leadership (i.e., integrity, charisma, inspirational, and visionary) and universal condemnation of other attributes (i.e., irritability, noncooperativeness, egocentric, being a loner, ruthlessness, and dictatorial) as inhibiting effective leadership; however, they also found that endorsement of other attributes varied significantly along cultural lines.[24]

---

[24] See generally Den Hartog, D.N., R.J. House, P.J. Hanges, S.A. Ruiz-Quintanilla, P.W. Dorfman, I.A Abdalla, and B.E. Akande. 1999. "Culture specific and Cross-Culturally Generalizable Implicit Leadership Theories: Are Attributes of Charismatic/Transformational Leadership Universally Endorsed?." *Leadership Quarterly* (Special issue: Charismatic and Transformational Leadership: Taking Stock of the Present and Future (Part I)) 10, no. 2, pp. 219–56. See also Dorfman, P.W., P.J. Hanges, and F.C. Brodbeck. 2004. "Leadership Prototypes and Cultural Variation: The Identification of Culturally Endorsed Implicit Theories of Leadership." In Culture, Leadership and Organizations: The GLOBE Study of 62 Societies, eds. R. House, P. Hanges, M. Javidan, P. Dorfman and V. Gupta. Thousand Oaks: Sage. ("charismatic/value-based" leadership was more likely to be endorsed in societies where cultural values included strong in-group collectivism and humane orientation, two of the cultural dimensions assessed in the GLOBE project). For further discussion of the debate regarding "universality" and "cultural contingency", see Chapter 3 of this publication.

CHAPTER 3

Universality Versus Cultural Contingency

Introduction

One of the fundamental goals of cross-cultural research relating to leadership is to determine whether attributes of leadership are perceived in the same way—positively or negatively—across all societal cultures (i.e., universally) or whether the perception of those attributes varied across the range of societal cultures ("culturally contingent"). The universalistic perspective is based on the proposition that although there are probably some differences across cultures with respect to leadership in general there are more similarities such that it is appropriate to expect that leaders around the world will rely upon a common toolkit of management practices and structures. Proponents of this view point to a variety of factors that they believe support their position including common technological imperatives and industrial logic and the emergence of global technologies and institutions,[1] as well as arguments that factors such as heredity and personality traits place universal constraints on how items such as culture and training can change how leaders think and act.[2] They also argue that

---

[1] Carl, D.E., and M. Javidan. 2001. "Universality of Charismatic Leadership: A Multi-Nation Study." Paper presented at the Academy of Management Proceedings.

[2] See, e.g., Johnson, A.M., P.A. Vernon, M. Molson, J.A. Harris, and K.L. Jang. 1998. "Born to Lead: A Behavior Genetic Investigation of Leadership Ability." Paper presented at the Society for Industrial Organization Psychology, Dallas, TX. (40 to 50 percent of variance in leadership behaviors of monozygotic twins could be attributed to heritability); and Bass, B.M. 1997. "Does the Transactional-Transformational Leadership Paradigm Transcend Organizational and National Boundaries?" *American Psychologist* 52, no. 2, pp. 130–39 (leadership requires a disposition to be "influential", a trait that arguably transcends cultural boundaries and also is difficult to "train").

forces of modernization and globalization are fueling a movement toward cultural congruence with respect to organizational and business practices and that leaders everywhere are now more concerned with dealing with contingencies that supersede cultural factors including larger and more complex organizations, rapidly changing technologies, designing and implementing strategies that are increasingly global, and coping with environmental instabilities that impact all countries at the same time.[3] As for those studies that claim to have identified observable differences across cultural boundaries, the "universalists" argue that in many instances those findings are due to research design limitations, unmatched sampling, and the like and that the actual level of the "pure" influence of cultural factors on leadership is probably negligible and insignificant.[4] In contrast, supporters of the cultural contingency position believe strongly that "the values, beliefs, norms, and ideals that are embedded in a culture affect leadership behavior and goals, as well as structure, culture, and strategies of organizations."[5]

Initial interviews with managers from various countries elicited responses that suggested to the researchers involved in the Global Leadership and Organizational Behavior Effectiveness ("GLOBE") project that culture was indeed an important factor in whether or not a particular leadership "attribute," or "style," would be effective with followers in a particular society. The GLOBE researchers set out to formally examine universality versus cultural contingency in more detail by identifying a

---

[3] Kerr, C. 1983. *The Future of Industrial Societies: Convergence or Continuing Diversity.* Cambridge, MA: Harvard University Press; and Blyton, P. 2001. "The General and the Particular in Cross-National Comparative Research." *Applied Psychology: An International Review* 50, no. 4, pp. 590–95.

[4] Zagoršek, H. September 2004. "Assessing the Impact of National Culture on Leadership: A Six Nation Study." https://researchgate.net/publication/320274490_Leadership_A_Global_Survey_of_Theory_and_Research

[5] Id. See also, e.g., Newman, K.L., and S.D. Nollen. 1996. "Culture and Congruence: The Fit Between Management Practices and National Culture." *Journal of International Business Studies* 27, no. 4, pp. 753–80 ("National culture is a central organizing principle of employees' understanding of work, their approach to it, and the way in which they expect to be treated. National culture implies that one way of action or one set of outcomes is preferable to another.").

large number of possible attributes of leaders and polling respondents around the world about whether these attributes contributed to the effectiveness of a leader or inhibited the ability of a leader to be effective and successful. The survey was intended to address the long-standing debate surrounding the following three key research questions:

- Are there one or more attributes that are universally perceived as contributors to outstanding leadership—if present these attributes would be considered to be "universal positive leader attributes"?
- Are there one or more attributes that are universally perceived as inhibitors of outstanding leadership—if present these attributes would be considered to be "universal negative leader attributes"?
- Are there one or more attributes that have an effect that is "culture specific," meaning that in some societies they are perceived as contributors to outstanding leadership while in other societies they are perceived as inhibitors of outstanding leadership—if present these attributes would be considered to be "culturally contingent leadership attributes"?

The leadership questionnaires designed by the GLOBE researchers included over 100 behavioral and attribute descriptors that the survey designers hypothesized as either contributing to a person's ability to be an outstanding leader or inhibiting a person's ability to be an outstanding leader. Each of the participants (i.e., thousands of middle managers from hundreds of organizations distributed among over 60 countries) were asked to rate each of the descriptors on a scale of 1 to 7 with a rating of "1" meaning that the behavior or attribute greatly inhibiting a person from being an outstanding leader and a rating of "7" meaning that the behavior or attribute greatly contributing to a person being an outstanding leader.[6]

---

[6] House, R.J., P.J. Hanges, M. Javidan, P.W. Dorfman, and V. Gupta. 2004. *Culture, Leadership, and Organizations: The GLOBE Study of 62 Societies.* Thousand Oaks CA: Sage.

While universality was a long-debated topic there was frequent disagreement about the standards that should be applied in forging an objective and workable definition of "universal." Recognizing this issue the GLOBE researchers set a fairly high bar for "universal endorsement." For example, an attribute could not be included among the universal positive leader attributes unless each of the following two requirements were satisfied: (1) at least 95 percent of the societal averages of the scores for that attribute had to exceed a mean of 5 on a scale going from 1 at the lowest to 7 at the highest and (2) the grand mean score on a world-wide basis for that attributes, including all of the societal cultures, had to exceed 6 on the 1-to-7 measurement scale. The requirements were necessarily different yet similar for inclusion among the universal negative leader attributes—(1) at least 95 percent of the societal averages of the scores for that attribute had to be less than a mean of 3 on the 1-to-7 measurement scale and (2) the grand mean score on a worldwide basis for that attributes, including all of the societal cultures, had to be less than 3 on the 1-to-7 scale. In order for an attribute to be "culturally contingent" it had to have societal average scores that were both above and below the midpoint of 4.[7]

As they approached the issue of effective leadership behaviors the GLOBE researchers relied heavily on a body of research known as "implicit leadership theory," which is based on the proposition that individuals around the world, regardless of their societal or cultural environment, gradually develop a set of beliefs regarding behaviors and characteristics of leaders beginning from a very early age and that as they grow older these beliefs become so engrained that they are often applied without any conscious awareness by the individual (i.e., they become "implicit").[8] One of the important things to understand about implicit leadership theory is that the "followers," rather than the "leaders," set

---

[7] Id. at 677–679.

[8] For further discussion of implicit leadership theories, see Schyns, B., and J. Meindl., eds. 2005. *Implicit Leadership Theories: Essays and Explorations.* Charlotte, NC: Information Age Publishing. and Lord, R.G., and K.J. Maher. 1991. *Leadership and Information Processing: Linking Perceptions and Performance.* Boston: Unwin-Everyman.

the rules and determine the characteristics that distinguish leaders from non-leaders and the leadership styles that separate effective and ineffective leaders.[9] A second key element of all these is the assumption that individuals within an interacting group—a society, a community, an organization, or a team—share similar implicit leadership theories because they typically share other things that contribute to a common "view of the world" including their general environment, recent experiences, challenges and successes, core values, education, religious beliefs, and the like. Testing this assumption was one of the main initial goals of the GLOBE researchers as they attempted to collect and present evidence that each organizational or societal culture would have its own specific ideas and beliefs regarding leadership styles and behaviors including what attributes are considered to be acceptable and effective and what attributes are considered to be impediments to effective leadership and thus unacceptable.[10]

Again, it is important to emphasize that, while the leadership "attributes" identified by the GLOBE researchers were important to the extent that they could be analyzed as "facilitators" or "inhibitors" of effective leadership, the attributes should not be confused with leadership itself. Identification of the attributes as "universal" or "culturally contingent" provides useful guidance to those seeking to "lead" within organizations, regardless of the level at which they are operating. Specifically, leaders everywhere should strive for those "universal" attributes that facilitate

---

[9] The GLOBE researchers explained the major assertions of implicit leadership theory as follows: "Leadership qualities are attributed to individuals, and those persons are accepted as leaders, on the basis of the degree of fit, or congruence, between the leader behaviors they enact and the implicit leadership theory held by the attributers. Implicit leadership theories constrain, moderate, and guide the exercise of leadership, the acceptance of leaders, the perception of leaders as influential, acceptable, and effective, and the degree to which leaders are granted status and privileges." See House, R.J., P. Hanges, S. Ruiz-Quintanilla, P. Dorfman, M. Javidan and M. Dickson. 1999. "Cultural Influences on Leadership and Organizations." *Advances in Global Leadership*, 171–233, 1 Vol. Greenwich, CT: JAI Press, Inc.

[10] Grove, C.N. 2005. "Leadership Style Variations Across Cultures: Overview of GLOBE Research Findings." Grovewell LLC: Grovewell.com/GLOBE. http://grovewell.com/pub-GLOBE-leadership.html (accessed December 31, 2018).

leadership effectiveness, such as being trustworthy, planning ahead, being positive and motivating, building confidence, being communicative, and being a coordinator and team integrator. At the same time, all leaders should steer clear of the "universal impediments" to their effectiveness, including being a loner and asocial, being noncooperative and irritable, and being dictatorial. The cultural context should determine whether or not other "culturally contingent" attributes described in the following, such as individualism, status consciousness, or risk-taking, would be effective for a leader in a specific cultural context.[11]

Universal Positives

The GLOBE researchers identified the following 22 attributes that satisfied the requirements for classification as one of the "universal positives"[12]:

Encouraging
Positive
Dynamic
Motive arouser
Confidence builder
Motivational
Communicative
Informed
Coordinator
Team builder
Trustworthy
Just
Honest

---

[11] For further discussion of leadership "attributes" identified by the GLOBE researchers, see Javidan, M., P.W. Dorfman, M.S. de Luque, and R. House. February 2006. "In the Eye of the Beholder: Cross Cultural Lessons in Leadership from Project GLOBE." *Academy of Management Perspectives* 20, no. 1, pp. 67–90.

[12] House, R.J., P.J. Hanges, M. Javidan, P.W. Dorfman, and V. Gupta., eds. 2004. *Culture, Leadership, and Organizations: The GLOBE Study of 62 Societies.* Thousand Oaks CA: Sage. Table 21.2 at 677.

Foresight
Plans ahead
Effective bargainer
Win-win problem solver
Dependable
Intelligent
Decisive
Administratively skilled
Excellence-oriented

It should not be forgotten that while an attribute might be universally endorsed and appreciated the steps that a leader needs to take in order to express these attributes successfully and effectively may vary significantly between societies based on their specific dominant cultural dimensions. For example, a leader is considered to be "decisive" in the United States if he or she makes quick and approximate decisions; however, in countries such as France and Germany the approved and expected process for decisiveness among leaders includes much higher levels of deliberation and precision than in the United States.[13]

While the results of the GLOBE study are the primary focus of the current discussion, it should be noted that several studies using relatively small groups of countries, three to five, from different parts of the world also identified universal support within those groups for various leadership attributes such as leadership supportiveness, contingent reward, charisma, participative leadership, supportive leadership, directive leadership, low neuroticism, and high extroversion.[14]

---

[13] Hoppe, M. 2007. "Culture and Leader Effectiveness: The GLOBE Study." September 2007, http://www.inspireimagineinnovate.com/PDF/GLOBEsummary-by-Michael-H-Hoppe.pdf (accessed December 31, 2018)

[14] See Dorfman, P.W., J.P. Howell, S. Hibino, J.K. Lee, U. Tate, and A. Bautista. 1997. "Leadership in Western and Asian countries: Commonalities and Differences in Effective Leadership Processes Across Cultures." *The Leadership Quarterly* 8, no. 3, pp. 233–74 (endorsement of leadership supportiveness, contingent reward and charisma in Japan, Korea, Mexico, Taiwan and the United States); Mehta, R., T. Larsen, B. Rosenbloom, J. Mazur, and P. Polsa. 2001. "Leadership and Cooperation in Marketing Channels: A Comparative Empirical Analysis

Universal Negatives

The GLOBE researchers identified the following eight attributes that satisfied the requirements for classification as one of the "universal negatives"[15]:

Loner
Asocial
Noncooperative
Irritable
Non-explicit
Dictatorial
Egocentric
Ruthless

Again, as is the case with the universal positive attributes listed earlier, the perception of whether particular behaviors express one of the universal negatives will vary between societies based on their specific dominant cultural dimensions. For example, the threshold for acting what is perceived negatively as "dictatorial" may be much higher in strong power distance societies where followers are more conditioned to firm and authoritative leadership practices while followers in lower power distance societies could be expected to be much more sensitive to autocratic or arbitrary actions by persons in a position to exercise control over them.[16]

---

of the USA, Finland and Poland." *International Marketing Review* 18, no. 6, pp. 633–67 (endorsement of participative, supportive and directive leadership); and Silverthorne, C. 2001. "Leadership Effectiveness and Personality: A Cross-Cultural Evaluation." *Personality and Individual Differences* 30, no. 2, pp. 303–09 (endorsement of low neuroticism and high extroversion in China, Thailand and the United States).

[15] House, R.J., P.J. Hanges, M. Javidan, P.W. Dorfman, and V. Gupta., eds. 2004. *Culture, Leadership, and Organizations: The GLOBE Study of 62 Societies.* Thousand Oaks CA: Sage. Table 21.3 at 678.

[16] Hoppe, M.H. 2007. "Culture and Leader Effectiveness: The GLOBE Study." September 2007, http://inspireimagineinnovate.com/PDF/GLOBEsummary-by-Michael-H-Hoppe.pdf (accessed December 31, 2018).

Culturally Contingent Attributes

One of the many important contributions of the GLOBE project to cross-cultural research in general, as well as the study of cross-cultural leadership in particular, was the evidence to support a finding that a leader's effectiveness is determined in large part by the context in which he or she is operating and the societal and organizational cultural values and beliefs of those persons following the leader.

The GLOBE researchers identified the following 35 attributes that satisfied the requirements for classification as one of the "culturally contingent leadership attributes." The list of these attributes along with the lowest and highest societal average score for those attributes is as follows[17]:

Able to anticipate (3.84—6.51)	Intuitive (3.72—6.47)
Ambitious (2.85—6.73)	Logical (3.89—6.58)
Autonomous (1.63—5.17)	Micromanager (1.60—5.00)
Cautious (2.17—5.78)	Orderly (3.81—6.34)
Class conscious (2.53—6.09)	Procedural (3.03—6.10)
Compassionate (2.69—5.56)	Provocateur (1.38—6.00)
Cunning (1.26—6.38)	Risk-taker (2.14—5.96)
Domineering (1.60—5.14)	Ruler (1.66—5.20)
Elitist (1.61—5.00)	Self-effacing (1.85—5.23)
Enthusiastic (3.72—6.44)	Self-sacrificial (3.00—5.96)
Evasive (1.52—5.67)	Sensitive (1.96—6.35)
Formal (2.12—5.43)	Sincere (3.99—6.55)
Habitual (1.93—5.38)	Status-conscious (1.92—5.77)
Independent (1.67—5.32)	Subdued (1.32—6.18)

[17] House, R.J., P.J. Hanges, M. Javidan, P.W. Dorfman, and V. Gupta, eds. 2004. *Culture, Leadership, and Organizations: The GLOBE Study of 62 Societies.* Thousand Oaks CA: Sage. Table 21.4 at 679. See also Den Hartog, D.N., R.J. House, P.J. Hanges, S.A. Ruiz-Quintanilla, P.W. Dorfman, I.A. Abdalla, and B.E. Akande. 1999. "Culture Specific and Cross-Culturally Generalizable Implicit Leadership Theories: Are Attributes of Charismatic/Transformational Leadership Universally Endorsed?" *Leadership Quarterly* (Special issue: Charismatic and Transformational Leadership: Taking Stock of the Present and Future (Part I) 10, no. 2, pp. 219–56).

Indirect (2.16—4.86)	Unique (3.47—6.06)
Individualistic (1.67—5.10)	Willful (3.06—6.48)
Intragroup competitor (3.00—6.49)	Worldly (3.48—6.18)
Intragroup conflict avoider (1.84—5.69)	

When reviewing the range of scores it is important to remember that a score of 1 meant that the attribute greatly inhibited outstanding business leadership and a score of 7 meant that the attribute greatly contributed to outstanding business leadership. For example, attitudes regarding the attribute of ambition were culturally contingent with mean scores across all of the societal cultures included in the survey running from 2.85 to 6.73 on a scale on which a score of 1 meant that ambition greatly inhibits outstanding business leadership and a score of 7 meant that ambition greatly contributes to outstanding business leadership. Similarly, attitudes regarding the attribute of cunning were culturally contingent with mean scores across all of the societal cultures included in the survey running from 1.26 to 6.38 on a scale on which a score of 1 meant that being cunning greatly inhibits outstanding business leadership and a score of 7 meant that being cunning greatly contributes to outstanding business leadership.

The range of societal average scores for each of the culturally contingent leadership attributes can be explained, in part, by the cultural characteristics of the various societies. For example, attitudes toward risk-taking by leaders, which has a range of 2.14 to 5.96, will likely be significantly impacted by a society's position on the continuum for the cultural dimension of uncertainty avoidance and followers in strong uncertainty avoidance societies will understandably have misgiving about leaders who appear to be behaving and managing in what locals perceive as an excessively risky manner.[18] Similarly, the effectiveness of certain leadership attributes will vary depending upon the feelings with a society regarding what is appropriate with respect to showing and expressing emotions. In "affective" societies people show their emotions and

---

[18] Hoppe, M.H. 2007. "Culture and Leader Effectiveness: The GLOBE Study." September 2007, http://inspireimagineinnovate.com/PDF/GLOBEsummary-by-Michael-H-Hoppe.pdf (accessed December 31, 2018).

appreciate outwardly enthusiastic leaders who communicate using vivid and temporal expressions of emotion. In contrast, people tended to hide or manage their emotions in more "neutral" societies and present themselves in a manner that was more composed and subdued.[19]

Additional Studies

Recognition and identification of culturally contingent leadership attributes created a large and intriguing reservoir for additional research to understand more fully why certain attributes are perceived differently across societies. One illustration is the examination by Aditya and House of the characteristics of leaders that represented a need for "interpersonal acumen" and their comparison of how different cultures rated these characteristics as contributors to outstanding leadership.[20] Among the characteristics examined were cunning, indirect communication, evasive behaviors, and sensitivity and the contrasts between societies were quite interesting. For example, cunning was cited by leaders in Columbia as contributing to outstanding leadership while leaders in Switzerland viewed cunning, or behaving in a sly or deceitful fashion, as inhibiting outstanding leadership. Cultural differences were also apparent when examining the feelings of leaders on the other characteristics. Another factor related to interpersonal acumen is "communication style" and leaders must be mindful of how followers in a particular culture expect to receive

---

[19] Den Hartog, D.N., R.J. House, P.J. Hanges, S.A. Ruiz-Quintanilla, P.W. Dorfman, I.A. Abdalla, and B.E. Akande. 1999. "Culture Specific and Cross-Culturally Generalizable Implicit Leadership Theories: Are Attributes of Charismatic/Transformational Leadership Universally Endorsed?" *Leadership Quarterly* (Special issue: Charismatic and Transformational Leadership: Taking Stock of the Present and Future (Part I)) 10, no. 2, pp. 219–56. See also Trompenaars, F., and C. Hampden-Turner. 1997. *Riding the Waves of Culture: Understanding Cultural Diversity in Business*, 2nd ed. London: Nicholas Breale. (describing researching confirming that displays of emotion may be interpreted as a lack of control or weakness).

[20] Aditya, R., and R.J. House. 2002. "Interpersonal Acumen and Leadership Across Cultures: Pointers from the GLOBE Study." In *Multiple Intelligences and Leadership*, eds. R. Riggio and S. Murphy, Mahwah, NJ: Erlbaum.

information and direction from those in authority. Hofstede's power distance dimension is relevant to this issue and it has been suggested that communication is mostly one-way, top to bottom, in high power distance societies and that it is expected that leaders will know more than their subordinates and that input from subordinates will neither be solicited nor welcomed.[21]

The results of other studies seemed to support the proposition of cultural contingency, although the research also confirmed that the effect of a much wider array of leadership attributes is culturally contingent[22]:

- A study of managerial skills in seven European countries and the United States identified two skills—"drive for results" and "analyze issues"—as universally recognized as being critical for success; however, several other skills were not endorsed across the board and overall the study provided limited support for the universality of leadership skill dimensions.[23]
- A study of midlevel managers in the United States, China, and Thailand partially supported universality by finding the effective leaders in each of the countries shared low neuroticism and high extroversion; however, the relationship between three other personality factors—high agreeableness, high

---

[21] See also Javidan, M., and R.J. House. 2001. "Cultural Acumen for the Global Manager: Lessons from Project GLOBE." *Organizational Dynamics* 29, no. 4, pp. 289–305.

[22] Based in part on summaries of the work of various cross-cultural leadership researchers appearing in Dickson, M.W., D.N. Den Hartog, and J.K. Mitchelson. 2003. "Research on Leadership in a Cross-Cultural Context: Making progress, and Raising New Questions." *The Leadership Quarterly* 14, no. 6, pp. 729–68, 733–34.

[23] See Robie, C., K. Johnson, D. Nilsen, and J. Fisher Hazucha. 2001. "The Right Stuff: Understanding Cultural Differences in Leadership Performance." *Journal of Management Development* 20, no. 7, pp. 639–50. Another study involving European managers, as well as managers from the United States, identified several other attributes and skills associated with effective leadership including valuing personal influence, cooperation and acceptance of rules and procedures established by an external authority. See Lesley, J.B., and E. Van Velsor. 1998. *A Cross-National Comparison of Effective Leadership and Teamwork: Toward a Global Workforce.* Greensboro, NC: Center for Creative Leadership.

conscientiousness, and high openness to experience—and effectiveness was culturally contingent.[24]

- Researchers studying managers and professionals in Japan, Korea, Mexico, Taiwan, and the United States found endorsement of three leadership behaviors of supervisors in every country—leader supportiveness, contingent reward, and charismatic leadership; however, the effects of three other behaviors—participative leadership, directive leadership, and contingent punishment—were culturally contingent in different ways. For example, contingent punishment only worked well in the United States, participative leadership only had positive effects in Korea and the United States, and directive leadership was the preferred approach in Mexico and Taiwan.[25]

As research continues and more and more attention is paid to non-Western countries[26] it appears that a consensus is growing that both

---

[24] See Silverthorne, C. 2001. "Leadership Effectiveness and Personality: A Cross Cultural Evaluation." *Personality and Individual Differences* 30, no. 2, pp. 303–09. High agreeableness and high conscientiousness correlated with effectiveness in the United States and China but not in Thailand and a correlation between high openness to experience and effectiveness was found only in the United States.

[25] See Dorfman, P.W., J.P. Howell, S. Hibino, J.K. Lee, U. Tate and A. Bautista. 1997. "Leadership in Western and Asian Countries: Commonalities and Differences in Effective Leadership Processes Across Cultures." *The Leadership Quarterly* 8, no. 3, pp. 233–74.

[26] One of the main criticisms of much of the research conducted in the area of cross-cultural studies has been that it has had a Western bias and fails to recognize culture specific non-Western cultural models. For example, relatively little work has been done to build new models from the unique vantage point of a non-Western culture and many of the studies of non-Western cultures are conducted primarily to assess whether one or more elements of a Western cultural model might be applicable in different contexts (e.g., a set of behaviors known to occur in Western countries is selected in advance and then research is done using a sample of Western and non-Western countries). Dickson, M.W., D.N. Den Hartog, and J.K. Mitchelson. 2003. "Research on Leadership in a Cross-Cultural Context: Making Progress, and Raising new Questions." *The Leadership Quarterly* 14, no. 6, pp. 72968, 734.

the simple universal and culture contingent perspectives are relevant to cross-cultural studies and, in fact, there has been a decided decline in the volume of research focusing primarily on identifying simple universals. Some studies indicate that some specified leadership behaviors achieve universal acceptance while others are endorsed in only certain cultures.[27] Other studies conclude that there are universally accepted behaviors but that their effectiveness in a particular context depends on applying them in ways that are specifically tailored to national cultural values and certain behaviors, while widely deployed, are used more frequently in some cultural settings than others.[28] Assuming these findings have some validity the challenge for leaders is to not only assess the universality of a particular behavior but to also acknowledge that even "universals" must be applied in a culturally specific manner in order to achieve optimal effectiveness. In fact, the state of affairs from a research perspective has been fairly summarized in the following passage by M.W. Dickson et al.:

> ... we have begun to recognize that variform and variform functional universals can be simultaneously universal and culturally contingent in a predictable way, as when the variation in the enactment of a common characteristic or the strength of a

---

[27] See, e.g., Bass, B.M. 1990. *Bass and Stodgill's Handbook of Leadership*, 3rd ed. New York, NY: Free Press. (study of two Western and three Asian countries found that while leader supportiveness and charisma, two behaviors generally associated with transformational leadership, appeared to be universally endorsed in all five countries only the Western countries had a positive reaction to two other transformational leadership behaviors: participativeness and directiveness. See also Dorfman, P.W., and J.P. Howell, Hibino, S., J.K. Lee, U. Tate, and A. Bautista. 1997. "Leadership in Western and Asian countries: Commonalities and Differences in Effective Leadership Processes Across Cultures." *Leadership Quarterly* 8, no. 3, pp. 233–67 (arguing that research indicates that commonalities and differences do exist across cultures with respect to effective leadership processes).

[28] See, e.g., Boehnke, K., N. Bontis, J. DiStefano, and A. DiStefano. 2003. "Transformational Leadership: An Examination of Cross-Cultural Differences and Similarities." *Leadership and Organization Development Journal* 24, no. 1, pp. 5–15 (team building behaviors used more frequently in the United States than in the Far East).

common relationship is determined by measurable characteristics of the cultures.[29]

Research activities now focus on identifying differences between cultures with respect to values, characteristics, and relationships that conform to or can be explained by the various cultural dimensions that have been suggested and which are subsequently described and elsewhere in this publication.[30]

---

[29] Dickson, M.W., D.N. Den Hartog, and J.K. Mitchelson. 2003. "Research on Leadership in a Cross-Cultural Context: Making Progress, and Raising New Questions." *The Leadership Quarterly* 14, no. 6, pp. 729–68, 734.

[30] The interest in and acceptance of cultural dimensions has grown along with the volume of information that has been collected regarding managerial practices and leadership styles in non-Western countries that have grown to challenge the economic supremacy of the United States and other Western countries. For example, paternalism is a leadership style that is valued in many emerging countries and thus must be recognized and understood even if it is not widely endorsed by management consultants advising businesses in the United States. See Dorfman, P., and J. Howell. 1988. "Dimensions of National Culture and Effective Leadership Patterns." *Advances in International Comparative Management* 3, no. 1, pp. 127–50.

CHAPTER 4

GLOBE Project Leadership Theory Dimensions

Introduction

The researchers involved in the Global Leadership and Organizational Behavior Effectiveness ("GLOBE") project identified a large number of potential "attributes" of organizational leaders and polled respondents around the world to determine whether these attributes contributed to the effectiveness of a leader or inhibited the ability of a leader to be effective and successful.[1] Based on statistical analysis of the responses the GLOBE researchers identified 21 "primary leadership dimensions" (sometimes called "first order factors") that all of the societal cultures in the survey appeared to agree were contributors to either effective or ineffective leadership. These dimensions are included in the following table ranked from the most universally desirable to the least universally desirable based on their "world mean," which is the average of the mean scores for that dimension for all of the societal cultures on the 1-to-7 measurement scale[2]:

Integrity (6.07)	Humane orientation (4.78)
Charismatic/inspirational (6.07)	Status consciousness (4.34)
Charismatic/visionary (6.02)	Conflict inducer (3.97)
Performance-oriented (6.02)	Procedural (3.87)
Team integrator (5.88)	Autonomous (3.85)

---

[1] For detailed discussion of the various leadership attributes identified and assessed by the GLOBE researchers, see the chapter on "Universality versus Cultural Contingency" in this publication.

[2] House, R.J., P.J. Hanges, M. Javidan, P.W. Dorfman, and V. Gupta., eds. 2004. *Culture, Leadership, and Organizations: The GLOBE Study of 62 Societies*, 131. Thousand Oaks CA: Sage.

Decisive (5.80)	Face-saver (2.92)
Administratively competent (5.76)	Nonparticipative (2.66)
Diplomatic (5.49)	Autocratic (2.65)
Team collaborative (5.46)	Self-centered (2.17)
Charismatic/self-sacrificial (5.0)	Malevolent (1.80)
Modesty (4.98)	

It is important to emphasize that the list of primary leadership dimensions is not a list of attributes of an outstanding leader—in fact several of the dimensions/attributes on the list, particularly those with a "world mean" score below 3, are included because of widespread belief that they can significantly impair a leader's ability to influence, motivate, and enable his or her subordinates to contribute to the success of the organization that the leader oversees.

It is also important to understand that each of the primary leadership dimensions represents a bundling of two to four of the larger number of original attributes identified by the GLOBE researchers. For example, specific attributes of a leader who is "administratively competent" would include things such as orderly, administratively skilled, organized, and being a good administrator. Another illustration would be the attributes for "decisive" including willful, decisive, logical, and intuitive. A "face saver" is indirect, avoids negatives, and is evasive.[3]

The GLOBE researchers used further statistical analysis to identify the primary leadership dimension to which each of the 22 universal positives listed previously had the strongest relationship. The list of universal positives and corresponding primary leadership dimensions is as follows[4]:

Universally positive attributes	Primary leadership dimension
Encouraging	Charismatic/inspirational
Positive	Charismatic/inspirational
Dynamic	Charismatic/inspirational

---

[3] A full list of the 21 dimensions and the associated attributes can be found in House, R.J., P.J. Hanges, M. Javidan, P.W. Dorfman, and V. Gupta., eds. 2004. *Culture, Leadership, and Organizations: The GLOBE Study of 62 Societies*, 131. Thousand Oaks CA: Sage, Table 8.4 at 131.

[4] Id., Table 21.2 at 677.

Universally positive attributes	Primary leadership dimension
Motive arouser	Charismatic/inspirational
Confidence builder	Charismatic/inspirational
Motivational	Charismatic/inspirational
Communicative	Team integrator
Informed	Team integrator
Coordinator	Team integrator
Team builder	Team integrator
Trustworthy	Integrity
Just	Integrity
Honest	Integrity
Foresight	Charismatic/visionary
Plans ahead	Charismatic/visionary
Effective bargainer	Diplomatic
Win-win problem solver	Diplomatic
Dependable	Malevolent (reverse score)
Intelligent	Malevolent
Decisive	Decisiveness
Administratively skilled	Administratively competent
Excellence-oriented	Performance-oriented

It is interesting to note that of the 22 attributes more than half of them were strongly linked to three of the primary leadership dimensions—charismatic/inspirational (6), team integrator (4), and integrity (3). This finding provides support for the proposition that these three dimensions and their associated attributes are widely endorsed across all societal cultures as contributing to acceptable and effective leadership behavior.

The GLOBE researchers used further statistical analysis to identify the primary leadership dimension to which each of the eight universal negatives listed earlier had the strongest relationship. The list of universal negatives and corresponding primary leadership dimensions is as follows[5]:

Universally negative attributes	Primary leadership dimensions
Loner	Self-protective
Asocial	Self-protective

---

[5] Id., Table 21.3 at 678.

Universally negative attributes	Primary leadership dimensions
Noncooperative	Malevolent
Irritable	Malevolent
Non-explicit	Face-saver
Dictatorial	Autocratic
Egocentric	None
Ruthless	None

The GLOBE researchers grouped the 21 primary leadership dimensions previously discussed into six culturally endorsed leadership theory dimensions based on further statistical analysis and explained them as follows: "These dimensions are summary indices of the characteristics, skills, and abilities culturally perceived to contribute to, or inhibit, outstanding leadership."[6] The researchers noted that these dimensions can be thought of as being somewhat similar to what laypersons refer to as "leadership styles" and others have referred to the dimensions as "global leadership dimensions," "global leader behaviors," or "second order factors." The following table describes the six culturally endorsed leadership theory dimensions using the applicable primary leadership dimensions (with the exception of "autonomous," which is described using questionnaire items) and also includes the lowest and highest societal average score for that dimension on the 1-to-7 measurement scale[7]:

Charismatic/value-based (4.5—6.5)	Team-oriented (4.8—6.2)
• Charismatic/visionary • Charismatic/inspirational • Charismatic/self-sacrificial • Integrity • Decisive • Performance-oriented	• Collaborative team orientation • Team integrator • Diplomatic • Malevolent (reverse-scored) • Administratively competent
Self-protective (2.6—4.6)	Participative (4.5—6.1)
• Self-centered • Status-conscious • Conflict inducer • Face-saver • Procedural	• Autocratic (reverse-scored) • Nonparticipative (reverse-scored)

---

[6] Id. at 675.

[7] Id., Table 21.1 at 676.

Humane (3.8—5.6)	Autonomous (2.3—4.7)
• Modesty	• Individualistic
• Humane orientation	• Independent
	• Autonomous
	• Unique

The GLOBE researchers concluded that the information collected during the survey provided evidence that the six global leadership dimensions of culturally endorsed implicit theories of leadership are significantly correlated with isomorphic dimensions of societal and organizational culture and that selected cultural differences strongly influence important ways in which people think about leaders and norms concerning the status, influence, and privileges granted to leaders.[8] The GLOBE researchers found strong support for their hypothesis that charismatic/value-based leadership would be universally endorsed. In addition, a strong correlation between team-oriented leadership and charismatic/value-based leadership was identified and team-oriented leadership was also universally endorsed. Humane and participative leadership dimensions were nearly universally endorsed; however, the endorsement of self-protective and autonomous leadership varied by culture.[9]

These six culturally endorsed leadership theory dimensions are just that dimensions or continua that can be used to evaluate how societal cultures from around the world perceive the acceptability and effectiveness of leadership behaviors. The dimensions are not intended to be universally accepted statements of what makes an outstanding leader nor do the dimensions provide practical guidance for leaders as to how they should act on a day-to-day basis so that their followers will recognize them as skilled practitioners of the attributes associated with the preferred behaviors. In fact, the way that these dimensions play out in the "real world" depends on a number of things including the cultural context and a good deal of the analysis undertaken in relation to the GLOBE project data is concerned with how the GLOBE cultural dimensions

---

[8] House, R.J., P. Hanges, S. Ruiz-Quintanilla, P. Dorfman, M. Javidan, and M. Dickson. 1999. "Cultural Influences on Leadership and Organizations." *Advances in Global Leadership*, 171–233, 1 Vol. Greenwich, CT: JAI Press, Inc.
[9] Id.

(i.e., performance orientation, power distance, assertiveness, etc.) relate to the leadership dimensions in the various societal clusters.[10]

The work of the GLOBE researchers has provided the foundation for a number of other culturally based models of leadership. For example, Muczyk and Holt prescribed that global leaders should adapt to changing economic conditions, particularly the growing intensity of globalization, by aligning their leadership styles and processes with cultural demands.[11] They went on to suggest a "global framework of leadership" by mapping the cultural determinants of leadership identified by the GLOBE researchers on to the following four "leadership dimensions" from the mid-range leadership theory proposed by Muczyk and Reimann based on observations of leadership behavior in North America:

- Consideration: Concern for people, good human relations, and treating subordinates with dignity, courtesy, and respect.
- Concern for production: Emphasis on challenging goals, achievement orientation, and high standards.
- Incentive for performance: Creating the strongest performance reward connection that is permitted within the applicable organizational constraints.
- Democracy-autocracy: Degree to which subordinates are involved in making significant day-to-day, work-related decisions, including goal setting.

Other scholars, such as Muczyk and Adler, had previously argued that in order to be "effective" leaders needed to score well on the first three

---

[10] Grove, C. 2005. "Leadership Style Variations Across Cultures: Overview of GLOBE Research Findings." *Grovewell LLC: Grovewell.com/GLOBE*, http://grovewell.com/pub-GLOBE-leadership.html (accessed December 31, 2018).

[11] Muczyk, J.P., and D.T. Holt. May 2008. "Toward a Cultural Contingency Model of Leadership." *Journal of Leadership & Organizational Studies* 14, no. 4, pp. 277–86, 278 and 281. (citing also Walumbwa, F.O., J.J. Lawler, and B.J. Avolio. 2007. "Leadership, Individual Differences, and Work-Related Attitudes: A Cross Cultural Investigation." *Applied Psychology: An International Review* 56, no. 2, pp. 212–30; and Nadler, N. 2002. *International Dimensions of Organizational Behavior*, 4th ed. Cincinnati, OH: Southwestern).

dimensions (i.e., consideration, concern for production, and incentive for performance), regardless of the situational context, and that the "prescription for these dimensions is a normative one."[12] They claimed that research confirmed that those firms that were "well-run" placed a premium on "sound human relations, high performance expectations and rewards tied to accomplishment." However, Muczyk and Holt argued that even among these "universals" differences could be found based on the cultural profile of the society within which the leader was acting.[13] For example, the level of consideration displayed by leaders could be expected to be higher in societies that scored high on femininity and humane orientation and low on assertiveness. Muczyk and Hold also recommended that appropriate "consideration" by leaders in high in-group collectivist societies would include involving family members of subordinates in employer-sponsored social gatherings.[14] With respect to "concern for production," leaders are likely to place a greater priority on this dimension when uncertainty avoidance is high and the society has an external environmental orientation and a short-term time orientation. Finally, Muczyk and Holt believed that reward systems strongly linked to individual performance would be effective in highly individualistic and performance-oriented societies while reward systems based on group- or organization-wide performance would be the preferred approach in societies that score high on collectivism and low on performance orientation.[15]

---

[12] Id. at 278 (citing Muczyk, J., and T. Adler. 2002. "An Attempt at a Consentience Regarding Formal Leadership." *Journal of Leadership and Organizational Studies* 9, no. 2, pp. 2–17).

[13] Id. at 282–83.

[14] Id. (citing Javidan, M., and R.J. House. 2001. "Cultural Acumen for the Global Manager: Lessons from Project GLOBE." *Organizational Dynamics* 29, pp. 289–305).

[15] With regard to evidence that organizations in different societal cultures use different reward systems, see Fischer, R., P.B. Smith, B. Richey, M.C. Ferreira, E.M.L. Assmar, J. Maes, and S. Stumpf. 2007. "How do Organizations Allocate Rewards?" *Journal of Cross-Cultural Psychology* 38, no. 1, pp. 3–18. See also Felix, C., S. Aparicio, and D. Urbano. 2018. "Leadership as a Driver of Entrepreneurship: An International Exploratory Study." https://emeraldinsight.com/doi/full/10.1108/JSBED-03-2018-0106 (accessed December 31, 2018).

Charismatic/Value-Based Leadership

The charismatic/value-based leadership theory dimension was of great interest to the GLOBE researchers given that it included a number of attributes that were universally praised as requirements for effective and outstanding leadership. This dimension reflects the ability to inspire, to motivate, and to expect high performance outcomes from others on the basis of firmly held core values.[16] The term "charisma" was defined as the power to inspire devotion and commitment for the group's goals and to produce power through infectious qualities of leadership and influence, involving a leader's aura, dynamism, and persuasiveness.[17] As noted earlier, the charismatic/value-based leadership dimension is statistically related to the largest number of primary leadership dimensions including extremely strong relationships to the charismatic/inspirational and charismatic/visionary dimensions along with the ties to charismatic/self-sacrificial, integrity, decisive, and performance-oriented. It has also been noted that a charismatic/value-based leader stresses high standards and innovation and strives to create a passion among his or her followers to perform and pursue a vision articulated by the leader.[18] It should not be forgotten, however, that while several attributes of charismatic/value-based leadership are universally endorsed as conditions for outstanding leadership the endorsement of many other attributes varied significantly along cultural lines and this means that charismatic or transformational leadership methods should be applied with cultural sensitivity by leaders and managers around the world.[19]

---

[16] House, R.J., P.J. Hanges, M. Javidan, P. Dorfman, and V. Gupta., eds. 2004. *Culture, Leadership, and Organizations: The GLOBE Study of 62 Societies.* Thousand Oaks CA: Sage. at 61 and 65.

[17] Id. at 500 and 515.

[18] Hoppe, M. 2007. "Culture and Leader Effectiveness: The GLOBE Study." September 2007, http://inspireimagineinnovate.com/PDF/GLOBEsummary-by-Michael-H-Hoppe.pdf (accessed December 31, 2018).

[19] See generally Den Hartog, D.N., R. House, P. Hanges, S. Ruiz-Quintanilla, P. Dorfman, I.A. Abdalla, and B.E. Akande. 1999. "Culture Specific and Cross-Culturally Generalizable Implicit Leadership Theories: Are Attributes of Charismatic/Transformational Leadership Universally Endorsed?" *Leadership Quarterly*

The range of the lowest to highest societal average score for this dimension on the 1-to-7 measurement scale was 4.5 to 6.5, which confirms that all of the societal cultures in the survey group believed that the charismatic/value-based leadership style contributed to outstanding leadership.[20] The societal clusters could be divided into three groups based on their relative enthusiasm for the charismatic/value-based leadership style. The group with the strongest preference for this style included the Anglo, Germanic Europe, Nordic Europe, Southern Asian, Latin Europe, and Latin America clusters; the middle group included the Confucian Asia, Sub-Saharan Africa, and Eastern Europe clusters; and the cluster with the lowest enthusiasm for the style was the Middle East (Arab) cluster.[21] The highest level of enthusiasm came from the Anglo cluster while the Middle East cluster had the lowest level of association between this dimension and outstanding leadership yet with a mean score within the cluster of 5.35 that was well above the midpoint of 4 on the 1-to-7 measurement scale.

The GLOBE researchers found a strong and positive correlation between high performance orientation and charismatic/value-based leadership and, in fact, this style is often referred to as "performance-oriented." The researchers commented:

[a] major finding was the large influence of the Performance Orientation cultural dimension as the most important predictor of the Charismatic/Value-Based leadership dimension. Societies and organizations that value excellence, superior performance, performance improvement, and innovation will likely seek leaders who

---

(Special issue: Charismatic and Transformational Leadership: Taking Stock of the Present and Future (Part I)) 10, no. 2, pp. 219–56.

[20] House, R.J., P.J. Hanges, M. Javidan, P.W. Dorfman, and V. Gupta., eds. 2004. *Culture, Leadership, and Organizations: The GLOBE Study of 62 Societies.* Thousand Oaks CA: Sage. Table 21.1 at 676.

[21] House, R.J., P.J. Hanges, M. Javidan, P.W. Dorfman, and V. Gupta., eds. 2004. *Culture, Leadership, and Organizations: The GLOBE Study of 62 Societies.* Thousand Oaks CA: Sage. Note that while clusters that are grouped together differ from clusters in other groups for the style there are no statistically significant differences between the clusters in a group.

exemplify Charismatic/Value-Based qualities, and such leaders are likely to be effective.[22]

High performance orientation societies have characteristics such as valuing training and development, valuing competitiveness and materialism, viewing formal feedback as necessary for performance improvement, valuing what one does more than who one is, and expecting direct and explicit communication.[23] The researchers advised that leaders can contribute to instilling a high value on performance orientation by setting ambitious goals, communicating high expectations for their subordinates, building their subordinates' self-confidence, and intellectually challenging their subordinates.[24] In addition, the researchers noted that members of high performance-oriented societies "seem to look to charismatic leaders who paint a picture of an ambitious and enticing future, but leave it to the people to build it."[25]

Charismatic/value-based leadership was also supported and endorsed among high in-group collectivist societies. In high in-group collectivist societies duties and obligations are important determinants of social behavior; a strong distinction is made between in-groups and out-groups; people emphasize relatedness with groups; the pace of life is slower; and love is assigned little weight in marriage.[26] In addition, charismatic/value-based leadership was supported and endorsed among high gender-egalitarian societies. In high gender-egalitarian societies there is an effort to minimize gender role differences and one finds more women in positions of authority, less occupational sex segregation, similar levels of educational attainment for males and females, and women being afforded greater decision-making roles in community affairs.[27] Specific leadership attributes perceived as effective in high gender-egalitarian societies

---

[22] Id. at 711.

[23] Id. at 245.

[24] Id. at 277.

[25] Id. at 278.

[26] Id. at 454.

[27] Id. at 359.

included foresight, enthusiasm, self-sacrifice, egalitarianism, delegation, and collective orientation.[28]

Charismatic leadership has sometimes been associated with a tendency and willingness of the leader to engage in "unconventional behavior" to motivate his or her followers.[29] It has been suggested, for example, that if leaders are willing and able to introduce "change" by adopting behaviors and attributes that are slightly different than what is traditionally expected and accepted under the dominant cultural values of the society they will be able to encourage innovation and improvements in performance among their followers provided that the disruption is not too radical.[30] While this concept sounds interesting and exciting and has some intuitive appeal there has been little evidence of support for the proposition in research studies that have been conducted to date.[31]

While the term "charismatic/value-based leadership" was chosen by the GLOBE researchers for inclusion in their list of culturally endorsed leadership theory dimensions, they noted that it was similar to transformational leadership, which has attracted great interest in the research community, and, in fact, one study focused on a leadership dimension explicitly referred to as "charismatic/transformational leadership" and noted that the results of the GLOBE survey provided evidence for the proposition that several attributes of charismatic/transformational leadership are universally endorsed as conditions for outstanding leadership

---

[28] Description of findings derived from Dickson, M.W., D.N. Den Hartog, and J. Mitchelson. 2003. "Research on Leadership in a Cross-Cultural Context: Making Progress, and Raising New Questions." *Leadership Quarterly* 14, no. 6, pp. 729–69, 746.

[29] See, e.g., Conger, J.A., and R.N. Kanungo. 1987. "Toward a Behavioral Theory of Charismatic Leadership in Organizational Settings." *Academy of Management Review* 12, no. 4, pp. 637–47.

[30] House, R.J., P. Hanges, and S. Ruiz-Quintanilla. 1997. "GLOBE: The Global Leadership and Organizational Behavior Effectiveness Research Program." *Polish Psychological Bulletin* 28, no. 3, pp. 215–54.

[31] Dickson, M.W., D.N. Den Hartog, and J.K. Mitchelson. 2003. "Research on Leadership in a Cross-Cultural Context: Making Progress, and Raising New Questions." *Leadership Quarterly* 14, no. 6, pp. 729–69, 746.

while at the same time the endorsement of many other attributes varied significantly along cultural lines.[32]

Bass has been a strong advocate of the position that the transactional-transformational leadership paradigm is universal and "transcends organizational and national boundaries" and has supported his arguments with results from research conducted on a wide array of organizations around the world in several different sectors including business, education, the military, the government, and the independent sector.[33] For example, Bass cited research supporting the effectiveness of transformational leadership in India, Japan, New Zealand, and Singapore as evidence that the transactional-transformational leadership paradigm transcended organizational and national boundaries.[34] Others took issue with Bass on the basis that his arguments regarding the cross-cultural popularity of transformational versus transactional leadership were based primarily on one-country studies carried out in a single cultural context. Another study of the impact of transformational leadership on teachers' commitment to change found similarities in North America and Hong Kong; however, the magnitude of the impact was much less among teachers in Hong Kong.[35] This finding is consistent with the work of other

---

[32] See generally Den Hartog, D.N., R.J. House, P.J. Hanges, S.A. Ruiz-Quintanilla, P.W. Dorfman, I.A. Abdalla, and B.E. Akande. 1999. "Culture Specific and Cross-Culturally Generalizable Implicit Leadership Theories: Are Attributes of Charismatic/Transformational Leadership Universally Endorsed?" *Leadership Quarterly* (Special issue: Charismatic and Transformational Leadership: Taking Stock of the Present and Future (Part I)) 10, no. 2, pp. 219–56.

[33] Ardichvili, A., and K.P. Kuchinke. 2002. "Leadership Styles and Cultural Values Among Managers and Subordinates: A Comparative Study of Four Countries of the Former Soviet Union, Germany and the US." *Human Resource Development International* 5, no. 1, pp. 99–117, 102 (citing Bass, B.M. 1997. "Does the Transactional-Transformational Paradigm Transcend Organizational and National Boundaries?" *American Psychologist* 52, no. 2, pp. 130–39).

[34] See Bass, B.M. 1997. "Does the Transactional-Transformational Leadership Paradigm Transcend Organizational and National Boundaries?" *American Psychologist* 52, no. 2, pp. 130–39.

[35] Yu, H., K. Leithwood, and D. Jantzi. 2002. "The Effects of Transformational Leadership on Teachers' Commitment to Change in Hong Kong." *Journal of Educational Administration* 40, nos. 4/5, pp. 368–90.

researchers who have examined the idea that while behaviors embodying transformational leadership are meaningful in all cultural contexts their enactment is demonstrably different depending on whether the context is Eastern or Western.[36] In addition, researchers compared managers and employees working in the United States and Germany for the same telecommunications company to identify cultural differences with respect to the use and appreciation of transformational and transactional leadership styles and found that while U.S. employees had higher levels of charisma and inspirational motivation than their German colleagues there were no other significant differences between the two cultural groups on any other transformational or transactional measures. The study also provided evidence that charisma and inspirational motivation could be predicted by the Hofstede's cultural dimensions of masculinity, individualism, and long-term orientation.[37] Finally, in their study of four former countries of the Soviet Union (Georgia, Kazakhstan, Kyrgyzstan, and Russia) Ardichvili and Kuchinke found that the two leadership behaviors with the highest scores in those countries—"inspirational motivation" and "contingent reward"—came from both the transformational and transactional leadership styles, an indication that elements of both styles were being used in those countries concurrently.[38]

---

[36] See Spreitzer, G., K. Perttula, and K. Xin. 2018. "Traditionality Matters: An Examination of the Effectiveness of Transformational Leadership in the U.S. and Taiwan." http://webuser.bus.umich.edu/spreitze/traditionalitymatters.pdf (accessed December 31, 2018). See also Jung, D.I., B.M. Bass, and J. Sosik. 1995. Bridging Leadership and Culture: A Theoretical Consideration of Transformational Leadership and Collectivist Cultures. The Journal of Leadership Studies 2, no. 4, pp. 3–18. (suggesting that transformational leadership is generalizable but that it is more important in societies that can be categorized as "collectivist" since followers in those societies are more comfortable with the recommended focus of transformational leaders on collective mission, goals and responsibilities).

[37] Kuchinke, K. 1999. "Leadership and Culture: Work-Related Values and Leadership Styles Among One Company's U.S. and German Telecommunication Employees." *Human Resource Development Quarterly* 10, no. 2, pp. 135–54.

[38] Ardichvili, A., and K.P. Kuchinke. 2002. "Leadership Styles and Cultural Values Among Managers and Subordinates: A Comparative Study of Four Countries of the Former Soviet Union, Germany and the US." *Human Resource Development International* 5, no. 1, pp. 99–117, 113. For further discussion of

Participative Leadership

The GLOBE researchers explained that the participative leadership theory dimension reflected the degree to which managers involve others in making and implementing decisions. As previously noted, this dimension is statistically related to two primary leadership dimensions (both reverse-scored): autocratic and nonparticipative. It has also been noted that the participative leadership style emphasizes delegation and equality.[39] The range of the lowest to highest societal average score for this dimension on the 1-to-7 measurement scale was 4.5 to 6.1, which confirms that all of the societal cultures in the survey group believed that the participative leadership style contributed to outstanding leadership.[40] The societal clusters could be divided into three groups based on their relative enthusiasm for the participative leadership style. The group with the strongest preference for this style included the Germanic Europe, Anglo, and Nordic Europe clusters; the middle group included the Latin Europe, Latin America, and Sub-Saharan Africa clusters; and the group with the lowest enthusiasm for the style included the Eastern Europe, Southern Asian, Confucian Asia, and Middle East (Arab) clusters.[41] The highest level of enthusiasm came from the Germanic Europe cluster (5.86) while the Middle East

---

charismatic leadership, see Veiss, S. 2016. "Charismatic, Transformational, and Servant Leadership in the United States, Mexico, and Croatia." *International Journal of Business and Social Research* 6, no. 12, p. 2164; and Charismatic Leadership Guide: Definition, Qualities, Pros & Cons, Examples (December 2016), https://www.cleverism.com/charismatic-leadership-guide (accessed December 31, 2018).

[39] Hoppe, M. September 2007. "Culture and Leader Effectiveness: The GLOBE Study." September 2007, http://inspireimagineinnovate.com/PDF/GLOBEsummary-by-Michael-H-Hoppe.pdf (accessed December 31, 2018).

[40] House, R., P.J. Hanges, M. Javidan, P.W. Dorfman, and V. Gupta., eds. 2004. *Culture, Leadership, and Organizations: The GLOBE Study of 62 Societies.* Thousand Oaks CA: Sage. Table 21.1 at 676.

[41] House, R.J., P.J. Hanges, M. Javidan, P.W. Dorfman, and V. Gupta., eds. 2004. *Culture, Leadership, and Organizations: The GLOBE Study of 62 Societies.* Thousand Oaks CA: Sage. Note that while clusters that are grouped together differ from clusters in other groups for the style there are no statistically significant differences between the clusters in a group.

cluster had the lowest level of association between this dimension and outstanding leadership yet with a mean score within the cluster of 4.97 that was well above the midpoint of 4 on the 1-to-7 measurement scale.

The participative leadership style was supported and endorsed among high gender-egalitarian societies.[42] In high gender-egalitarian societies there is an effort to minimize gender role differences and one finds more women in positions of authority, less occupational sex segregation, similar levels of educational attainment for males and females, and women being afforded greater decision-making roles in community affairs.[43] Specific leadership attributes perceived as effective in high gender-egalitarian societies included foresight, enthusiasm, self-sacrifice, egalitarianism, delegation, and collective orientation.[44] In addition, support for the participative leadership style was positively correlated to performance orientation.[45]

On the other hand, the participative leadership style was strongly disapproved of among high uncertainty societies.[46] Characteristics of high uncertainty avoidance societies (i.e., societies that attempt to reduce stressful ambiguity through creation and enforcement of norms, rules, and procedures) include use of formality in interactions with others, maintenance of orderly and meticulous records, reliance on formalized policies and procedures, strong resistance to change, and preference for moderate and carefully calculated risks.[47] It should also be noted that

---

[42] Dorfman, P.W., P.J. Hanges, and F.C. Brodbeck. 2004. "Leadership Prototypes and Cultural Variation: The Identification of Culturally Endorsed Implicit theories of Leadership." In *Supra Note_*.R. House et al.

[43] Id. at 359.

[44] Description of findings derived from Dickson, M.W., D.N. Den Hartog, and J.K. Mitchelson. 2003. "Research on Leadership in a Cross-Cultural Context: Making Progress, and Raising New Questions." *Leadership Quarterly* 14, no. 6, pp. 729–69, 746.

[45] Dorfman, P.W., P.J. Hanges, and F.C. Brodbeck. 2004. "Leadership Prototypes and Cultural Variation: The Identification of Culturally Endorsed Implicit Theories of Leadership." In *Culture, Leadership, and Organizations: The GLOBE Study of 62 Societies*, eds. R. House, P. Hanges, M. Javidan, P. Dorfman and V. Gupta, Thousand Oaks CA: Sage.

[46] Id.

[47] Id. at 618.

the intensity of endorsement of the participative leadership style within a country was negatively correlated with the strength of assertiveness in that country.[48]

The GLOBE researchers reported finding some statistical evidence of a negative correlation between the participative leadership style and high power distance,[49] which would seem to be logically expected given that high power distance societies are characterized by class differentiation and hoarding of resources and information by the limited few vested with power and status; however, the correlation was not sufficiently strong for the researchers to cite it as one of their major findings with respect to the relationships between the cultural and leadership style dimensions. The participative leadership style was endorsed in GLOBE country clusters where small power distance was the norm—Anglo, Germanic, and Nordic European—while it was not embraced as strongly in country clusters where large power distances were more prevalent such as the Confucian Asian, East European, Middle Eastern, and Southern Asian clusters.[50] Other studies of smaller groups of countries have also provided support for the notion that participative leadership is only effective in the countries with smaller power distance and not particularly effective in the other larger power distance countries.[51]

Another study provided support for the relationship between cultural values and the preferred level of subordinate involvement (i.e., "participation") in decisions that managers are required to make regarding strategy and operations. Specifically, managers were more likely to tap into the experience of subordinates and allow them to participate in decisions when the societal cultural values included high individualism, cultural

---

[48] Id.

[49] Id.

[50] Id.

[51] See Dorfman, P.W., J.P. Howell, S. Hibino, J.K. Lee, U. Tate, and A. Bautista. 1997. "Leadership in Western and Asian countries: Commonalities and Differences in Effective Leadership Processes Across Cultures." *The Leadership Quarterly* 8, no. 3, pp. 233–74; and Bu, N., T.J. Craig, and T.K. Peng. 2001. "Acceptance of Supervisory Direction in Typical Workplace Situations: A Comparison of US, Taiwanese and PRC Employees." *International Journal of Cross Cultural Management* 1, no. 2, pp. 131–52.

autonomy, egalitarianism, low power distance, harmony, and femininity; however, supervisorial authority and formal rules played much bigger roles in the making of decisions—and subordinate participation was minimal or nonexistent—in societies characterized by collectivism, cultural embeddedness, hierarchy, power distance, mastery, and masculinity.[52]

One study using the GLOBE data to explore attitudes regarding various leadership attributes in Europe found that participative leadership was endorsed as strongly contributing to effective leadership in France and in countries in the North/West European region; however, countries in the South/East European region were lukewarm on that style.[53] Several other studies using relatively small groups of countries, three to five, from different parts of the world identified universal support within those groups for leadership attributes such as leadership supportiveness, contingent reward, charisma, participative leadership, supportive leadership, directive leadership, low neuroticism, and high extroversion.[54]

A participatory leadership style is related to the democracy-autocracy dimension in the "global framework of leadership" model suggested by

---

[52] Smith, P.B., M.F. Peterson, S.H. Schwartz. 2002. "Cultural Values, Sources of Guidance, and their Relevance to Managerial Behavior—A 47-Nation Study." *Journal of Cross-Cultural Psychology* 33, no. 2, pp. 188–208.

[53] Broadbeck, F.C., M. Frese, S. Akerblom, G. Audia, G. Bakacsi, H. Bendova, and P. Castel. 2000. "Cultural Variation of Leadership Prototypes Across 22 European Countries." *Journal of Occupational and Organizational Psychology* 73, no. 1, pp. 1–29.

[54] See Dorfman, P.W., J.P. Howell, S. Hibino, J.K. Lee, U. Tate, and A. Bautista. 1997. "Leadership in Western and Asian countries: Commonalities and Differences in Effective Leadership Processes Across Cultures." *The Leadership Quarterly* 8, no. 3, pp. 233–74 (endorsement of leadership supportiveness, contingent reward and charisma in Japan, Korea, Mexico, Taiwan and the United States); Mehta, R., T. Larsen, B. Rosenbloom, J. Mazur, and P. Polsa. 2001. "Leadership and Cooperation in Marketing Channels: A Comparative Empirical Analysis of the USA, Finland and Poland." *International Marketing Review* 18, no. 6, pp. 633–67 (endorsement of participative, supportive and directive leadership); and Silverthorne, C. 2001. "Leadership Effectiveness and Personality: A Cross-Cultural Evaluation." *Personality and Individual Differences* 30, no. 2, pp. 303–09. (Endorsement of low neuroticism and high extroversion in China, Thailand and the United States.)

Muczyk and Holt. Muczyk and Adler believed that democracy-autocracy was "situational" and required great attention to alignment with a large range of societal culture dimensions, including power distance, individualism-collectivism, masculinity-femininity, uncertainty avoidance, perceived role hierarchy, environmental orientation, and the acceptability of bypassing the chain of command (i.e., rigidity of hierarchy).[55] Muczyk and Holt observed that "democratic leadership" with respect to making decisions and setting goals "may be suited for cultures that are low on power distance, high on individualism and femininity, low on uncertainty avoidance and characterized by internal environmental orientation" and "might also be suitable in societies whose members have a low regard for hierarchy and an inclination to bypass the chain of command."[56] On the other hand, Muczyk and Holt speculated that "autocratic leadership" might be more appropriate in societies "that are high in power distance, collectivism, masculinity, and uncertainty avoidance and that are characterized by external environmental orientation" and in societies "whose members have a high regard for hierarchy and are reluctant to bypass the chain of command."[57] The observations made by Muczyk and Holt were similar to those made by Hofstede, who argued that large power distance and collectivism were closely related and typically associated

---

[55] Muczyk, J.P., and T. Adler. 2002. "An Attempt at a Consentience Regarding Formal Leadership." *Journal of Leadership and Organizational Studies* 9, no. 2, pp. 2–17. Muczyk and Adler actually distinguished between the style used for making decisions and setting goals, the democracy-autocracy continuum, and the amount of follow-up or directive behavior associated with execution of a decision that has been made or attainment of a goal that has been established, the directive-participative continuum. As a result, rather than leaders being "democratic" or "autocratic", Muczyk and Adler identified four "leadership types" by combining the extremes of the two continuums: directive autocrat, permissive autocrat, directive democrat and permissive democrat.

[56] Muczyk, J.P., and D. Holt. May 2008. "Toward a Cultural Contingency Model of Leadership." *Journal of Leadership & Organizational Studies* 14, no. 4, pp. 277–86, 282.

[57] Id.

with developing countries while small power distance and high individualism were closely related and typically associated with industrialized countries.[58]

Autonomous Leadership

The GLOBE researchers described the autonomous leadership style dimension as referring to independent, individualistic, and self-centric leadership.[59] As noted earlier, this dimension was statistically related to one of the primary leadership dimensions that itself was named "autonomous." The range of the lowest to highest societal average score for this dimension on the 1-to-7 measurement scale was 2.3 to 4.7, which means that most societies were either neutral about the impact of autonomous leadership behaviors on the effectiveness of the leader or felt that such behaviors had a moderately inhibiting impact on leader effectiveness.[60] While it was possible for several leadership styles to divide the societal clusters into groups based on statistically based differences in their relative enthusiasm for the style this was not possible for the autonomous leadership style as there were no statistically significant differences across all the clusters. The highest level of enthusiasm for the autonomous leadership style came from the Eastern Europe and Germanic Europe clusters, each of which had mean scores within the cluster that were slightly above the midpoint of 4 on the 1-to-7 measurement scale (i.e., Eastern Europe (4.20) and Germanic Europe (4.16)), while the strongest sentiment

---

[58] Hofstede, G. Fall. 1983. "The Cultural Relativity of Organizational Practices and Theories." *Journal of International Business Studies*, p. 82. For further discussion of practical aspects of implementing a participative leadership style, see Root, G. 2018. "The Advantages of Participative Leadership." https://smallbusiness.chron.com/advantages-participative-leadership-17629.html (accessed June 29, 2018).

[59] Hoppe, M. 2007. "Culture and Leader Effectiveness: The GLOBE Study." September 2007, http://inspireimagineinnovate.com/PDF/GLOBEsummary-by-Michael-H-Hoppe.pdf (accessed December 31, 2018).

[60] House, R.J., P.J. Hanges, M. Javidan, P.W. Dorfman, and V. Gupta., eds. 2004. *Culture, Leadership, and Organizations: The GLOBE Study of 62 Societies.* Thousand Oaks CA: Sage. Table 21.1 at 676.

against autonomous leadership as a contributor to effective leadership was found in the Sub-Saharan African, Middle Eastern, Latin European, and Latin American country clusters.[61]

Autonomous leadership was found to be strongly and positively correlated with high performance orientation; however, high institutional collectivist societies, which value group loyalty and expect group participation in the making of decisions, strongly disapproved of autonomous leadership style. Brodbeck et al. found that a leadership dimension that they also referred to as "autonomy" was perceived to be more prototypical of outstanding leadership in those European countries where autonomy was strong (i.e., the Germanic cluster, Georgia, and the Czech Republic) than in those countries where autonomy was weaker (i.e., the Anglo, Nordic, Central, Latin, and Near East European country clusters).[62]

Team-Oriented Leadership

The GLOBE researchers described the team-oriented leadership style dimension as emphasizing effective team building and implementation of a common purpose or goal among team members. As noted before, this

---

[61] Dorfman, P.W., P.J. Hanges, and F.C. Brodbeck. 2004. "Leadership Prototypes and Cultural Variation: The Identification of Culturally Endorsed Implicit Theories of Leadership." In *Culture, Leadership, and Organizations: The GLOBE Study of 62 Societies*, eds. R. House, P. Hanges, M. Javidan, P. Dorfman and V. Gupta, Thousand Oaks CA: Sage. The Latin America cluster had the lowest level of association between the autonomous leadership style and outstanding leadership yet with a mean score within the cluster below the mid-point of the measurement scale at 3.51.

[62] Brodbeck, F.C., M. Frese, S. Akerblom, G. Audia, G. Bakacsi, H. Bendova, and P. Castel. 2000. "Cultural Variation of Leadership Prototypes Across 22 European Countries." *Journal of Occupational and Organizational Psychology* 73, no. 1, pp. 1–29. It should be noted that Brodbeck et al. developed and tested leadership prototypes that differed from those used by the GLOBE researchers—Interpersonal Directness and Proximity, Autonomy and Modesty. For further discussion of autonomous leadership, see M. Stevenson, Autonomous Leadership and Ways to Encourage Autonomy in the Workplace (May 18, 2018), https://hrexchange-network.com/hr-talent-management/articles/autonomous-leadership-and-ways-to-encourage (accessed December 31, 2018).

dimension is statistically related to five primary leadership dimensions including collaborative team orientation, team integrator, diplomatic, administratively competent, and a reverse-scored malevolent. Team-oriented leaders are skilled in instilling and maintaining pride, loyalty, and collaboration among their followers.[63] The range of the lowest to highest societal average score for this dimension on the 1-to-7 measurement scale was 4.7 to 6.2, which confirms that all of the societal cultures in the survey group believed that the team-oriented leadership style contributed to outstanding leadership.[64] While it was possible for several leadership styles to divide the societal clusters into groups based on statistically based differences in their relative enthusiasm for the style this was not possible for the team-oriented leadership style as there were no statistically significant differences across all the clusters.[65] The highest level of enthusiasm for the team-oriented leadership style came from the Latin America cluster while the Middle East cluster had the lowest level of association between this style and outstanding leadership yet the mean score within the cluster of 5.47 was well above the midpoint of 4 on the 1-to-7 measurement scale.

The GLOBE researchers were mildly surprised to find that the team-oriented leadership style was supported and endorsed among high uncertainty avoidance societies.[66] Characteristics of high uncertainty avoidance societies (i.e., societies that attempt to reduce stressful ambiguity through creation and enforcement of norms, rules, and procedures) include use of formality in interactions with others, maintenance of orderly and meticulous records, reliance on formalized policies and procedures, strong resistance to change, and preference for moderate and carefully calculated risks.[67] The team-oriented leadership style was also supported and endorsed among high in-group collectivist societies.

---

[63] Hoppe, M. 2007. "Culture and Leader Effectiveness: The GLOBE Study." September 2007, http://inspireimagineinnovate.com/PDF/GLOBEsummary-by-Michael-H-Hoppe.pdf (accessed December 31, 2018).

[64] House, R.J., P.J. Hanges, M. Javidan, P.W. Dorfman, and V. Gupta., eds. 2004. *Culture, Leadership, and Organizations: The GLOBE Study of 62 Societies.* Thousand Oaks CA: Sage. Table 21.1 at 676.

[65] Id.

[66] Id at 712.

[67] Id. at 618.

In high in-group collectivist societies duties and obligations are important determinants of social behavior; a strong distinction is made between in-groups and out-groups; people emphasize relatedness with groups; the pace of life is slower; and love is assigned little weight in marriage. Finally, team-oriented leadership was perceived as being especially important for effective leadership in high uncertainty avoidance societies.[68]

Humane-Oriented Leadership

The GLOBE researchers described the humane-oriented leadership style dimension as reflecting patient, supportive, and considerate leadership as well as compassion, generosity, and concern for the well-being of others.[69] As noted earlier, this dimension is statistically related to two primary leadership dimensions—modesty and humane-oriented. Across all of the societal cultures this dimension was generally viewed positively as reflected by the fact that the range of the lowest to highest societal average score for this dimension on the 1-to-7 measurement scale was 3.8 to 5.6; however, the level of enthusiasm for humane-oriented leadership was not as high as it was for other leadership styles such as charismatic/value-based, team-oriented, and participative.[70] The societal clusters could be divided

---

[68] Dorfman, P.W., P.J. Hanges, and F.C. Brodbeck. 2004. "Leadership Prototypes and Cultural Variation: The Identification of Culturally Endorsed Implicit Theories of Leadership." In *Culture, Leadership, and Organizations: The GLOBE Study of 62 Societies*, eds. R. House, P. Hanges, M. Javidan, P. Dorfman and V. Gupta, Thousand Oaks CA: Sage. The strongest endorsement of team-oriented leadership was found in those clusters—Southern Asian, Confucian Asian and Latin American—where the scores of members on in-group collectivism, humane orientation and uncertainty avoidance were all high. With regard to team-oriented leadership, see also Rossberger, R.J., and D.E. Krause. February 2015. "Participative and Team-Oriented Leadership Styles, Countries' Education Level and National Innovation: The Mediating Role of Economic Factors and National Cultural Practices." *Cross-Cultural Research* 49, no. 1, p. 20.

[69] Hoppe, M. 2007. "Culture and Leader Effectiveness: The GLOBE Study." September 2007, http://inspireimagineinnovate.com/PDF/GLOBEsummary-by-Michael-H-Hoppe.pdf (accessed December 31, 2018).

[70] House, R.J., P.J. Hanges, M. Javidan, P.W. Dorfman, and V. Gupta., eds. 2004. *Culture, Leadership, and Organizations: The GLOBE Study of 62 Societies*. Thousand Oaks CA: Sage. Table 21.1 at 676.

into three groups based on their relative enthusiasm for the humane orientation leadership style. The group with the strongest preference for this style included the Southern Asian, Anglo, Sub-Saharan Africa, and Confucian Asia clusters; the middle group included the Germanic Europe, Middle East (Arab), Latin America, and Eastern Europe clusters; and the group with the lowest enthusiasm for the style included the Latin Europe and Nordic Europe clusters.[71] The highest level of support for the humane-oriented leadership style came from the Southern Asia cluster (5.38) while the Nordic Europe cluster had the lowest level of association between this style and outstanding leadership (4.42, just slightly above the midpoint of 4 on the 1-to-7 measurement scale).

The humane orientation leadership style was, not surprisingly, supported and endorsed by high humane orientation societies. In high humane orientation societies one finds the interests of others are important, people are motivated primarily by a need for belonging and affiliation, members of society feel that they are responsible for promoting the well-being of others, child labor is limited by public sanctions, and people are urged to be sensitive to all forms of racial discrimination.[72] The humane-oriented leadership style was also supported and endorsed among high uncertainty avoidance societies. Characteristics of high uncertainty avoidance societies (i.e., societies that attempt to reduce stressful ambiguity through creation and enforcement of norms, rules, and procedures) include use of formality in interactions with others, maintenance of orderly and meticulous records, reliance on formalized policies and procedures, strong resistance to change, and preference for moderate and carefully calculated risks.[73]

---

[71] House, R.J., P.J. Hanges, M. Javidan, P.W. Dorfman, and V. Gupta., eds. 2004. *Culture, Leadership, and Organizations: The GLOBE Study of 62 Societies.* Thousand Oaks CA: Sage. Note that while clusters that are grouped together differ from clusters in other groups for the style there are no statistically significant differences between the clusters in a group.

[72] Id. at 570.

[73] Id. at 618. See also Leonard, K. 2018. "Advantages & Disadvantages of People-Oriented Leadership Styles." June 30, 2018, https://smallbusiness.chron.com/advantages-disadvantages-peopleoriented-leadership-styles-10299.html (accessed December 31, 2018).

Self-Protective Leadership

The GLOBE researchers explained that the self-protective leadership style dimension focused on ensuring the safety and security of the individual or group member and was composed of items that reflected being status- and class-conscious, ritualistic, procedural, normative, secretive, evasive, indirect, self-centered, and asocial. The researchers commented, for example, that self-protective leaders may need to "protect themselves from acts of criticism and corruption," may want to insure "that they are not made into scapegoats for political ends," and may wish to "respond to humane considerations."[74] As previously noted, this dimension is statistically related to several of the aforementioned primary leadership dimensions including self-centered, status-conscious, conflict inducer, face-saver, and procedural.

Across all of the societal cultures this dimension was generally viewed neutrally as reflected by the fact that the range of the lowest to highest societal average score for this dimension on the 1-to-7 measurement scale was 2.5 to 4.6.[75] The societal clusters could be divided into three groups based on their relative enthusiasm for the self-protective leadership style. The group with the strongest preference for this style included the Middle East (Arab), Confucian Asia, Southern Asian, Latin America, and Eastern Europe clusters; the middle group included the Sub-Saharan Africa and Latin Europe clusters; and the group with the lowest enthusiasm for the style included the Anglo, Germanic Europe, and Nordic Europe clusters.[76] The highest level of support for self-protective leadership came

---

[74] House, R.J., P.J. Hanges, M. Javidan, P.W. Dorfman, and V. Gupta., eds. 2004. *Culture, Leadership, and Organizations: The GLOBE Study of 62 Societies.* Thousand Oaks CA: Sage, at 555.

[75] Id., Table 21.1 at 676.

[76] House, R.J., P.J. Hanges, M. Javidan, P.W. Dorfman, and V. Gupta, eds. 2004. *Culture, Leadership, and Organizations: The GLOBE Study of 62 Societies.* Thousand Oaks CA: Sage. Note that while clusters that are grouped together differ from clusters in other groups for the style there are no statistically significant differences between the clusters in a group. A study using the entire GLOBE dataset found that self-protective leadership was generally viewed as neutral or negative; however, there were significant cultural variations. In the Nordic Europe clusters,

from the Southern Asia cluster (3.83, just slightly below the midpoint of 4 on the 1-to-7 measurement scale) while the Nordic Europe cluster had the lowest level of association between this style and outstanding leadership at 2.72, a sign that societies in this cluster felt that self-protective behaviors inhibited effective leadership.

The self-protective leadership style was supported and endorsed among high uncertainty avoidance societies. Characteristics of high uncertainty avoidance societies (i.e., societies that attempt to reduce stressful ambiguity through creation and enforcement of norms, rules, and procedures) include use of formality in interactions with others, maintenance of orderly and meticulous records, reliance on formalized policies and procedures, strong resistance to change, and preference for moderate and carefully calculated risks.[77]

The self-protective leadership style was also supported and endorsed among high power distance societies. Characteristics of high power distance societies include differentiation of the society into classes, power being perceived as providing social order, limited upward social mobility, resources available only to a select few, and localized and hoarded information.[78] The researchers commented that "the high power distance values and practices of Asian societies are often associated with face-saving and status-consciousness, both of which are elements of the Self-Protective leadership dimension."[79]

---

as well as in the Germanic Europe cluster, attributes of self-protective leadership such as self-centered, status conscious, face saving and inducing conflict were perceived as extremely inhibiting effective leadership; however, the reaction to those attributes in countries in the Asian cultural clusters was much less hostile. See Dorfman, P.W., P.J. Hanges, and F.C. Brodbeck. 2004. "Leadership Prototypes and Cultural Variation: The Identification of Culturally Endorsed Implicit Theories of Leadership." In *Leadership, and Organizations: The GLOBE Study of 62 Societies Culture*, eds. R. House, P. Hanges, M. Javidan, P. Dorfman and V. Gupta, Thousand Oaks CA: Sage.

[77] House, R.J., P.J. Hanges, M. Javidan, P.W. Dorfman, and V. Gupta., eds. 2004. *Culture, Leadership, and Organizations: The GLOBE Study of 62 Societies.* Thousand Oaks CA: Sage. at 618.

[78] Id. at 536.

[79] Id. at 707.

The self-protective leadership was explored in detail by Brodbeck et al. in their study of cultural variation of leadership prototypes in Europe.[80] While those researchers borrowed significantly from the GLOBE project they chose to design and analyze three of their own leadership dimensions: interpersonal directness and proximity, autonomy, and modesty. The first dimension, interpersonal directness and proximity, was closely associated, albeit negatively, with several of the key attributes associated with self-protective leadership. Specifically, the researchers explained that interpersonal directness and proximity

> ... was shown to be most distinctively and negatively associated with Face Saver, comprising leadership attributes such as indirect, evasive, avoids negatives and face saving; with Self Centered, comprising the attributes, self interested, non-participative, loner and asocial; and with Administrative, comprising orderly organized and good administrator.

The researchers also noted that interpersonal directness and proximity

> ... was most distinctly and positively related with Inspirational, comprising for example enthusiastic, encouraging, confidence builder, morale booster and motive arouser; and with Integrity comprising for example, honest, sincere, just and trustworthy

In summary, label "directness" was the opposite of "face saving" (i.e., self-protective in the language of the GLOBE leadership dimensions). Their analysis of the data from all of the European countries led them to conclude that, in the Germanic, Anglo, and Nordic countries (most prominently in Finland), leadership attributes of interpersonal directness and proximity are perceived to be more prototypical of outstanding leadership than in South/East European countries and, in fact, this dimension

---

[80] Brodbeck, F.C., M. Frese, S. Akerblom, G. Audia, G. Bakacsi, H. Bendova, et al. 2000. "Cultural Variation of Leadership Prototypes Across 22 European Countries." *Journal of Occupational and Organizational Psychology* 73, no. 1, pp. 1–29.

mainly separated the South/East from North/West European countries.[81] This finding was roughly consistent with the GLOBE project—self-protective leadership was disapproved of in the Nordic Europe cluster yet endorsed among societies in the Eastern Europe cluster.[82]

Another study dealt with conflict inducement, which is one of the primary leadership dimensions associated with self-protective leadership. Specifically, Morris et al. studied the impact that cultural background might have on the preferences of managers from four countries—China, India, the Philippines, and the United States—with respect to conflict resolution styles and techniques.[83] The survey and accompanying analysis led to the conclusion that U.S. managers relied more heavily on a competing style of conflict resolution while Chinese managers were likely to choose and follow an avoiding conflict style. It has been suggested that this result can be linked to the finding that U.S. managers have higher achievement values than their managerial colleagues in China and that Chinese managers place a higher value on social conservatism (i.e., conformity and adherence to tradition) than U.S. managers.[84]

---

[81] Id.

[82] As noted earlier, the leadership profiles of the Eastern Europe and Nordic Europe clusters are strongly different from one another.

[83] Morris, M.W., K.Y. Williams, K. Leung, R. Larrick, M. Mendoza, D. Bhatnager, and J.C. Hu. 1998. "Conflict Management Style: Accounting for Cross-National Differences." *Journal of International Business Studies* 29, no. 4, pp. 729–47.

[84] China and the Philippines scored higher than India and the United States with respect to social conservatism and U.S. managers had higher achievement values than their managerial colleagues in China, India, and the Philippines. The scores of the countries with respect to the weight and respect given to conformity and tradition correlated with the finding that the value of power was rated much more highly by managers in China, India, and the Philippines than by managers in the United States.

CHAPTER 5

Cultural Dimensions and Leadership Attributes

Introduction

One of the most important byproducts of the Global Leadership and Organizational Behavior Effectiveness ("GLOBE") project was the identification and measurement of a set of cultural dimensions that could be used to facilitate analysis of the relationship between the cultural dimensions associated with a society and the preferences and dislikes of that society with respect to the attributes and behaviors of its leaders. For each of the cultural dimensions in their model the GLOBE researchers confirmed statistically significant associations with any of the culturally endorsed leadership theory dimensions they had identified based on the results of their study. The associations were made using cultural dimension values, not measurements of actual practice, because both cultural values and the leadership theory dimensions represent desired states with respect to culture and leadership attributes, respectively.[1] There were numerous such associations for each cultural dimension; however, the following sections generally cite only those associations that were classified as "highly significant" by the researchers and also describe the findings of a number of other researchers who have examined relationships between the broadly understood and accepted societal cultural dimensions and leadership styles, attributes, and behaviors.[2]

---

[1] House, R.J., P.J. Hanges, M. Javidan, P.W. Dorfman, and V. Gupta., eds. 2004. *Culture, Leadership, and Organizations: The GLOBE Study of 62 Societies.* Thousand Oaks CA: Sage. at 45.

[2] Id. at 702–708.

Uncertainty Avoidance

Characteristics of high uncertainty avoidance societies (i.e., societies that attempt to reduce stressful ambiguity through creation and enforcement of norms, rules, and procedures) include use of formality in interactions with others, maintenance of orderly and meticulous records, reliance on formalized policies and procedures, strong resistance to change, and preference for moderate and carefully calculated risks.[3] The GLOBE researchers found that the attributes associated with team-oriented leadership were perceived as being especially important for effective leadership in societies where uncertainty avoidance, as well as in-group collectivism and humane orientation, was all high such as the countries in the Southern Asian, Confucian Asian, and Latin American clusters, all of which strongly endorsed team-oriented leadership styles.[4] The GLOBE researchers also found that the general rule was that the intensity of endorsement of participative leadership within a country was negatively correlated with the strength of uncertainty avoidance, assertiveness, and power distance in that country.[5] The humane-oriented leadership style was also supported and endorsed among high uncertainty avoidance societies. Finally, the self-protective leadership style was supported and endorsed among high uncertainty avoidance societies. High uncertainty avoidance societies are preoccupied with alleviating the unpredictability of future events and thus it is not surprising that this leadership style is popular in such societies since being self-protective is one means to reduce uncertainty.[6]

Several other researchers have studied the relationship between uncertainty avoidance and preferred leadership attributes and strategies. One

---

[3] Id. at 618.

[4] Dorfman, P.W., P.J. Hanges, and F.C. Brodbeck. 2004. "Leadership Prototypes and Cultural Variation: The Identification of Culturally Endorsed Implicit Theories of Leadership." In *Culture, Leadership, and Organizations: The GLOBE Study of 62 Societies*, eds. R. House, P. Hanges, M. Javidan, P. Dorfman and V. Gupta, Thousand Oaks CA: Sage.

[5] Id.

[6] House, R.J., P.J. Hanges, M. Javidan, P.W. Dorfman, and V. Gupta., eds. 2004. *Culture, Leadership, and Organizations: The GLOBE Study of 62 Societies*, 707. Thousand Oaks CA: Sage.

study found that middle managers in different countries found variations in their opinions regarding the effectiveness of leadership attributes such as being habitual, procedural, risk-taking, able to anticipate, formal, cautious, and orderly.[7] Another study conducted of the actual behavior of managers in different countries found that as uncertainty avoidance levels rose managers tended to become more controlling and directive, less delegating, and less approachable.[8] This is consistent with research that found that managers in Germany, a high uncertainty avoidance country, expected their subordinates to be punctual and reliable while managers in Great Britain, a low uncertainty avoidance country, expected their subordinates to demonstrate resourcefulness and improvisation.[9]

Persons in high uncertainty avoidance societies were less open to "innovation champions" and "transformational leaders" and preferred that efforts to promote innovation were carried out through formal channel, rules, and procedures and in accordance with existing organizational norms. In contrast, in societies where uncertainty avoidance was lower there was greater acceptance and endorsement of radical innovation championing activities that included, if necessary, violation of existing organizational rules and regulations.[10]

Individualism/Collectivism

The GLOBE researchers broke Hofstede's individualism/collectivism dimension into institutional collectivism, which measured societal

[7] Den Hartog, D.N., R.J. House, P.J. Hanges, S.A. Ruiz-Quintanilla, P.W. Dorfman, I.A. Abdalla, and B.E. Akande. 1999. "Culture Specific and Cross-Culturally Generalizable Implicit Leadership Theories: Are Attributes of Charismatic/Transformational Leadership Universally Endorsed?" *Leadership Quarterly* (Special Issue: Charismatic and Transformational Leadership: Taking Stock of the Present and Future (Part I)) 10, no. 2, pp. 219–56.

[8] Offermann, L.R., and P.S. Hellmann. 1997. "Culture's Consequences for Leadership Behavior: National Values in Action." *Journal of Cross-Cultural Psychology* 28, no. 3, pp. 342–51.

[9] Stewart,R., J. Barsoux, A. Kieser, H. Ganter, and P. Walgenbach. 1994. *Managing in Britain and Germany*. London: St. Martin's Press/MacMillan Press.

[10] Shane, S. 1995. "Uncertainty Avoidance and the Preference for Innovation Championing Roles." *Journal of International Studies* 26, no. 1, pp. 47–68.

emphasis on collectivism, and in-group collectivism, which measured group (family and/or organization) collectivism. In high in-group collectivist societies duties and obligations are important determinants of social behavior; a strong distinction is made between in-groups and out-groups; people emphasize relatedness with groups; the pace of life is slower; and love is assigned little weight in marriage.[11] The GLOBE researchers found that the attributes associated with team-oriented leadership were perceived as being especially important for effective leadership in societies where in-group collectivism, as well as uncertainty avoidance and humane orientation, was all high such as the countries in the Southern Asian, Confucian Asian, and Latin American clusters, all of which strongly endorsed team-oriented leadership styles.[12] The enthusiasm for team-oriented leadership among high in-group collectivist societies is not surprising given the value that such societies place on pride, loyalty, and cohesiveness in their organizations or families.[13] Charismatic/value-based leadership was also supported and endorsed among high in-group collectivist societies such as the countries in the Anglo, Germanic, and Nordic culture clusters.[14] The GLOBE researchers found that high institutional collectivist societies, which value group loyalty and expect group participation in the making of decisions, strongly disapproved of autonomous leadership style.

It has been suggested that transformational leadership styles might be more successful in collectivist societies since persons in those societies are

---

[11] House, R.J., P.J. Hanges, M. Javidan, P. Dorfman, and V. Gupta., eds. 2004. *Culture, Leadership, and Organizations: The GLOBE Study of 62 Societies*, 454. Thousand Oaks CA: Sage.

[12] Dorfman, P.W., P.J. Hanges, and F.C. Brodbeck. 2004. "Leadership Prototypes and Cultural Variation: The Identification of Culturally Endorsed Implicit Theories of Leadership." In *Culture, Leadership, and Organizations: The GLOBE Study of 62 Societies*, eds. R. House, P. Hanges, M. Javidan, P. Dorfman and V. Gupta. Thousand Oaks CA: Sage.

[13] Id. at 712.

[14] Dorfman, P.W., P.J. Hanges, and F.C. Brodbeck. 2004. "Leadership Prototypes and Cultural Variation: The Identification of Culturally Endorsed Implicit Theories of Leadership." In *Culture, Leadership, and Organizations: The GLOBE Study of 62 Societies*, eds. R. House, P. Hanges, M. Javidan, P. Dorfman and V. Gupta. Thousand Oaks CA: Sage.

more willing to subordinate their own personal goals to the goals established for their organizations.[15] Jung et al. suggested that transformational leadership is generalizable but that it is more important in societies that can be categorized as "collectivist" since followers in those societies tend to identify with the goals of their leaders and the common purposes and objectives established for their group or organization would therefore be more comfortable with the recommended focus of transformational leaders on collective mission, goals, and responsibilities.[16] As for leadership styles in individualistic societies where persons are more concerned about themselves and motivated by individual achievement and rewards it would appear that short-term focused transactional leadership would be a more appropriate and effective approach.[17] Another study compared managers and employees working in the United States and Germany for the same telecommunications company to identify cultural differences with respect to the use and appreciation of transformational and transactional leadership styles and found that while U.S. employees had higher levels of charisma and inspirational motivation than their German colleagues there were no other significant differences between the two cultural groups on any other transformational or transactional measures. The study also provided evidence that charisma and inspirational motivation could be predicted by the cultural dimensions of masculinity, individualism, and long-term orientation.[18]

Several groups of researchers have used the horizontal/vertical distinctions within the individualism-collectivism continuum to examine topics

---

[15] See, e.g., Earley, P.C. 1999. "Playing Follow the Leader: Status-Determining Traits in Relation to Collective Efficacy Across Cultures." *Organizational Behavior and Human Decision Processes* 80, no. 3, pp. 192–212; and Triandis, H. 1995. *Individualism and Collectivism*. Boulder, CO: Westview Press.

[16] Jung, D.I., B.M. Bass, and J.J. Sosik. 1995. "Bridging Leadership and Culture: A Theoretical Consideration of Transformational Leadership and Collectivist Cultures." *The Journal of Leadership Studies* 2, pp. 3–18.

[17] Jung, D.I., and B.J. Avolio. 1999. "Effects of Leadership Style and Followers' Cultural Orientation on Performance in Group and Individual Task Conditions." *Academy of Management Journal* 42, no. 2, pp. 208–18.

[18] Kuchinke, K.P. 1999. "Leadership and Culture: Work-Related Values and Leadership Styles Among One Company's U.S. and German Telecommunication Employees." *Human Resource Development Quarterly* 10, no. 2, pp. 135–54.

related to leadership styles and practices.[19] For example, researchers studying and comparing the United States and Denmark determined that the
United States was more vertically oriented than Denmark while Denmark
was more horizontally oriented than the United States and suggested that
this could explain why Americans placed more emphasis on achievement,
displays of success, and setting and achieving goals than the Danes.[20]
Another study focusing on authoritarianism—deference to and respect
for authority—has found evidence of correlations between authoritarianism and vertical individualism and collectivism.[21] Triandis and Gelfand
also found vertical collectivists to be more authoritarian and traditional,
but also stressed sociability, while horizontal collectivists stressed sociability, interdependence, and hedonism. As for individualists, they found
that vertical individualists stressed competition and hedonism more than
horizontal individualists and that self-reliance was a trait that horizontal
individualists consistently found to be important.[22]

Humane Orientation

In high humane orientation societies one finds the interests of others are
important, people are motivated primarily by a need for belonging and
affiliation, members of a society feel that they are responsible for promoting the well-being of others, child labor is limited by public sanctions, and

---

[19] See also Dickson, M.W., D.N. Den Hartog, and J.K. Mitchelson. 2003.
"Research on Leadership in a Cross-Cultural Context: Making Progress, and
Raising New Questions." *Leadership Quarterly* 14, no. 6, pp. 729–69, 744 (noting that further research on the horizontal and vertical aspects of individualism
and collectivism would be useful since it is likely that different leadership traits
will be required to effectively lead and manage persons in each of the four groups).
[20] Nelson, M.R., and S. Shavitt. 2002. "Horizontal and Vertical Individualism
and Achievement Values: A Multimethod Examination of Denmark and the
United States." *Journal of Cross-Cultural Psychology* 33, no. 5, pp. 439–758.
[21] Kemmelmeier, M., E. Burnstein, K. Krumov, P. Genkova, C. Kanagawa, M.S.
Hirshberg, and K.A. Noels. 2003. "Individualism, Collectivism and Authoritarianism in Seven Societies." *Journal of Cross-Cultural Psychology* 34, no. 3,
pp. 304–22.
[22] Triandis, H.C., and M.J. Gelfand. 1998. "Converging Measurement of Horizontal and Vertical Individualism and Collectivism." *Journal of Personality and
Social Psychology* 74, no. 1, pp. 118–28, 119.

people are urged to be sensitive to all forms of racial discrimination.[23] The humane orientation leadership style was, not surprisingly, supported and endorsed by high humane orientation societies. The GLOBE researchers also found that the attributes associated with team-oriented leadership were perceived as being especially important for effective leadership in societies where humane orientation, as well as uncertainty avoidance and in-group collectivism, was all high such as the countries in the Southern Asian, Confucian Asian, and Latin American clusters, all of which strongly endorsed team-oriented leadership styles.[24] Finally, the level of support for charismatic/value-based leadership was likely to be higher in societies where cultural values included strong humane orientation and in-group collectivism such as the countries in the Anglo, Germanic, and Nordic culture clusters.[25]

Assertiveness

Conversational directedness is associated with assertiveness and is an important consideration in the communication techniques practiced by leaders. Leaders need to be mindful that attitudes differ among societies regarding the degree to which attributes such as "indirect," "evasive," and "intuitive" are considered to be important to outstanding leadership skills.[26] For example, while directness is valued and indirectness is perceived as socially undesirable in the United States societies such as

---

[23] House, R.J., P.J. Hanges, M. Javidan, P.W. Dorfman, and V. Gupta., eds. 2004. *Culture, Leadership, and Organizations: The GLOBE Study of 62 Societies,* 570. Thousand Oaks CA: Sage.

[24] Dorfman, P.W., P.J. Hanges and F.C. Brodbeck. 2004. "Leadership Prototypes and Cultural Variation: The Identification of Culturally Endorsed Implicit Theories of Leadership." In *Culture, Leadership, and Organizations: The GLOBE Study of 62 Societies,* eds. R. House, P. Hanges, M. Javidan, P. Dorfman and V. Gupta, Thousand Oaks CA: Sage.

[25] Id.

[26] Den Hartog, D.N., R.J. House, P.J. Hanges, S.A. Ruiz-Quintanilla, P.W. Dorfman, I.A. Abdalla, and B.E. Akande. 1999. "Culture Specific and Cross-Culturally Generalizable Implicit Leadership Theories: Are Attributes of Charismatic/Transformational Leadership Universally Endorsed?" *Leadership Quarterly* (Special issue: Charismatic and Transformational Leadership: Taking Stock of the Present and Future (Part I)) 10, no. 2, pp. 219–56.

Korea tend to be more indirect.[27] The general rule was that the intensity of endorsement of participative leadership within a country was negatively correlated with the strength of assertiveness, uncertainty avoidance, and power distance in that country.[28]

Power Distance

Characteristics of high power distance societies include differentiation of the society into classes, power being perceived as providing social order, limited upward social mobility, resources available only to a select few, and localized and hoarded information.[29] The general rule was that the intensity of endorsement of participative leadership within a country was negatively correlated with the strength of power distance.[30] The participative leadership style was endorsed in GLOBE country clusters where small power distance was the norm—Anglo, Germanic, and Nordic European—while it was not embraced as strongly in country clusters where large power distances were more prevalent such as the Confucian Asian, East European, Middle Eastern, and Southern Asian clusters.[31]

---

[27] Holtgraves, T. 1997. "Styles of Language Use: Individual and Cultural Variability in Conversational Indirectness." *Journal of Personality and Social Psychology* 73, no. 3,pp. 624–37. It has been suggested that indirectness in communication can be linked to "face management". See Brown, P., and S.C. Levinson. 1987. *Politeness: Some Universals in Language Usage.* Cambridge, UK: Cambridge University Press.

[28] Dorfman, P.W., P.J. Hanges, and F.C. Brodbeck. 2004. "Leadership Prototypes and Cultural Variation: The Identification of Culturally Endorsed Implicit theories of Leadership." In *Culture, Leadership, and Organizations: The GLOBE Study of 62 Societies,* eds. R. House, P. Hanges, M. Javidan, P. Dorfman and V. Gupta. Thousand Oaks CA: Sage.

[29] House, R.J., P. Hanges, M. Javidan, P. Dorfman, and V. Gupta, eds. 2004. *Culture, Leadership, and Organizations: The GLOBE Study of 62 Societies,* 536. Thousand Oaks CA: Sage.

[30] Dorfman, P.W., P.J. Hanges, and F.C. Brodbeck. 2004. "Leadership Prototypes and Cultural Variation: The Identification of Culturally Endorsed Implicit Theories of Leadership." In *Culture, Leadership, and Organizations: The GLOBE Study of 62 Societies,* eds. R. House, P. Hanges, M. Javidan, P. Dorfman and V. Gupta. Thousand Oaks CA: Sage.

[31] Id.

The findings of the GLOBE researchers have generally been confirmed by others. For example, one study that included Japan, Mexico, South Korea, Taiwan, and the United States concluded that participative leadership was only effective in the countries with the smaller power distance relative to the others—South Korea and the United States—and was not particularly effective in the other larger power distance countries.[32] Another study concluded that employees in larger power distance countries, such as China and Taiwan, were more likely to be willing to accept direction from supervisors without question than employees in smaller power distance countries such as the United States. Chinese employees were, however, sensitive to the alignment between the directions they received and company policies but as long as the directions were supported by policy they were not likely to condition their compliance with supervisorial instructions by their own assessment as to whether or not the directions were meritorious.[33] Finally, the finding that managers in lower power distance countries rely more on their interpersonal skills for communication and are seen as more approachable is consistent with the studies mentioned earlier.[34] Connerley and Pedersen have advised that leaders working in high power distance countries should not rely too much on

---

[32] See Dorfman, P.W., J.P. Howell, S. Hibino, J.K. Lee, U. Tate, and A. Bautista. 1997. "Leadership in Western and Asian Countries: Commonalities and Differences in Effective Leadership Processes Across Cultures." *The Leadership Quarterly* 8, no. 3, pp. 233–74. Job performance data from Mexico and the United States collected and analyzed in the same study led the researchers to conclude that only participative leadership had a direct and positive impact on job performance in the United States and that directive and supportive leadership did not have a positive impact in that country. The findings with regard to Mexico, a country with a much higher power distance index than the United States, were just the opposite and would indicate that leaders in Mexico are best advised to practice directive and supportive, rather than participative, leadership to elicit the best performance from subordinates.

[33] Bu, N., T.J. Craig, and T.K. Peng. 2001. "Acceptance of Supervisory Direction in Typical Workplace Situations: A Comparison of US, Taiwanese and PRC Employees." *International Journal of Cross Cultural Management* 1, no. 2, pp. 131–52.

[34] Offermann, L.R., and P.S. Hellmann. 1997. "Culture's Consequences for Leadership Behavior: National Values in Action." *Journal of Cross-Cultural Psychology* 28, no. 3, pp. 342–51.

participative practices, such as encouraging subordinates to provide opinions and solutions and participating in the making of decisions, since in those countries it is expected that the leaders will have all the answers and a leader might be perceived as weak or incompetent if he or she goes too far in including subordinates in management of the business.[35]

Power distance has also been associated with acceptance and effectiveness of a non-GLOBE leadership style—the directive and supportive leadership style, sometimes referred to as "paternalistic," which carries with it high levels of status orientation, support, and involvement by leaders in the nonwork lives of their subordinates.[36] One group of researchers found that directive leadership was likely to have a positive effect in terms of satisfaction and commitment of subordinates in larger power distance countries such as Mexico and Taiwan while not having a positive effect in countries with a smaller power distance such as Japan, South Korea, and the United States.[37] A number of other researchers have opined that paternalistic leadership is commonly found in developing countries, which tend not only to have larger power distances but also other cultural characteristics that may be conducive to accepting and embracing paternalistic leadership such as strong family bonds, a sense of fatalism, and the expectation among subordinates that their organizations will take care of them and their families.[38]

---

[35] Connerley, M.L., and P.B. Pedersen. 2005. Leadership in a Diverse and Multicultural Environment: Developing Awareness, Knowledge, and Skills, 46. Thousand Oaks, CA: Sage Publications.

[36] Dickson, M.W., D.N. Den Hartog, and J.K. Mitchelson. 2003. "Research on Leadership in a Cross-Cultural Context: Making Progress, and Raising New Questions." *Leadership Quarterly* 14, no. 6, pp. 729–69, 739.

[37] See Dorfman, P.W., J.P. Howell, S. Hibino, J.K. Lee, U. Tate, and A. Bautista. 1997. "Leadership in Western and Asian Countries: Commonalities and Differences in Effective Leadership Processes Across Cultures." *The Leadership Quarterly* 8, no. 3, pp. 233–74.

[38] Dickson, M.W., D.N. Den Hartog, and J.K. Mitchelson. 2003. "Research on Leadership in a Cross-Cultural Context: Making Progress, and Raising New Questions." *Leadership Quarterly* 14, no. 6, pp. 729–69, 739. See also Dorfman, P.W., and J.P. Howell. 1988. "Dimensions of National Culture and Effective Leadership Patterns." *Advances in International Comparative Management* 3,

The self-protective leadership style was also supported and endorsed among high power distance societies particularly those societies, many of which are found in Asia, where face-saving and status consciousness are important.[39]

Performance Orientation

High performance orientation societies have characteristics such as valuing training and development, valuing competitiveness and materialism, viewing formal feedback as necessary for performance improvement, valuing what one does more than who one is, and expecting direct and explicit communication.[40] The GLOBE researchers found a strong and positive correlation between high performance orientation and charismatic/value-based leadership and, in fact, this style is often referred to as "performance-oriented." The researchers noted that leaders can contribute to instilling a high value on performance orientation by setting ambitious goals, communicating high expectations for their subordinates, building their subordinates' self-confidence, and intellectually challenging their subordinates and that members of high performance-oriented societies "seem to look to charismatic leaders who paint a picture of an ambitious and enticing future, but leave it to the people to build it."[41] The GLOBE researchers also found support for the participative leadership

---

no. 1, 127–50; Dorfman, P.W., J.P. Howell, S. Hibino, J.K. Lee, U. Tate, and A. Bautista. 1997. "Leadership in Western and Asian Countries: Commonalities and Differences in Effective Leadership Processes Across Cultures." *The Leadership Quarterly* 8, no. 3, pp. 233–74; and Kanungo, R.N., and M. Mendonca. 1996. "Cultural Contingencies and Leadership in Developing Countries." *Research in the Sociology of Organizations* 14, pp. 263–95.

[39] The GLOBE researchers specifically commented that "the high power distance values and practices of Asian societies are often associated with face-saving and status-consciousness, both of which are elements of the Self-Protective leadership dimension." House, R.J., P.J. Hanges, M. Javidan, P.W. Dorfman, and V. Gupta. eds. 2004. *Culture, Leadership, and Organizations: The GLOBE Study of 62 Societies*, 707. Thousand Oaks CA: Sage.

[40] Id. at 245.

[41] Id. at 277–278.

style was positively correlated to performance orientation.[42] The GLOBE researchers found autonomous leadership to be strongly and positively correlated with high performance orientation.

Gender Egalitarianism

In high gender egalitarian societies there is an effort to minimize gender role differences and one finds more women in positions of authority, less occupational sex segregation, similar levels of educational attainment for males and females, and women being afforded greater decision-making roles in community affairs.[43] Specific leadership attributes perceived as effective in high gender egalitarian societies included foresight, enthusiasm, self-sacrifice, egalitarianism, delegation, and collective orientation.[44] Charismatic/value-based leadership was supported and endorsed among high gender egalitarian societies and specific leadership attributes perceived as effective in high gender egalitarian societies included foresight, enthusiasm, self-sacrifice, egalitarianism, delegation, and collective orientation.[45] Finally, support for participative leadership was positively correlated to gender egalitarianism and performance orientation.[46]

---

[42] Dorfman, P.W., P.J. Hanges, and F.C. Brodbeck. 2004. "Leadership Prototypes and Cultural Variation: The Identification of Culturally Endorsed Implicit Theories of Leadership." In *Culture, Leadership, and Organizations: The GLOBE Study of 62 Societies*, eds. R. House, P. Hanges, M. Javidan, P. Dorfman and V. Gupta. Thousand Oaks CA: Sage.

[43] House, R.J., P.J. Hanges, M. Javidan, P.W. Dorfman and V. Gupta., eds. 2004. *Culture, Leadership, and Organizations: The GLOBE Study of 62 Societies*, 359. Thousand Oaks CA: Sage.

[44] Description of findings derived from Dickson, M.W., D.N. Den Hartog, and J.K. Mitchelson. 2003. "Research on Leadership in a Cross-Cultural Context: Making Progress, and Raising New Questions." *Leadership Quarterly* 14, no. 6, pp. 729–69, 746.

[45] Id.

[46] Dorfman, P.W., P.J. Hanges, and F.C. Brodbeck. 2004. "Leadership Prototypes and Cultural Variation: The Identification of Culturally Endorsed Implicit theories of Leadership." In *Culture, Leadership, and Organizations: The GLOBE Study of 62 Societies*, eds. R. House, P. Hanges, M. Javidan, P. Dorfman and V. Gupta. Thousand Oaks CA: Sage.

CHAPTER 6

Theories and Studies of Culture and Leadership

GLOBE Researchers' Integrated Theory

The Global Leadership and Organizational Behavior Effectiveness ("GLOBE") study was arguably the most comprehensive analysis and assessment of universality and cultural congruence with respect to leadership and management practices and appeared to confirm that culture does indeed "matter" when it comes to identifying effective leadership styles and behaviors. An interesting and provocative by-product of the GLOBE project was the development of what the GLOBE researchers referred to as an "integrated theory" regarding the relationship between societal culture, leadership attitudes and behaviors, organizational culture, and leader acceptance and effectiveness that could be used as the basis for guiding future cross-cultural leadership research.[1] The GLOBE researchers explained that the central theoretical proposition of their integrated theory was that the attributes and entities that distinguish a given societal culture from other cultures are predictive of the practices of organizations and leader attributes and behaviors that are most frequently enacted, acceptable, and effective in that culture.[2] The integrated theory consists of the following propositions[3]:

---

[1] For a detailed discussion of the integrated theory, see House, R.J., N.S. Wright, and R.N. Aditya. 1977. "Cross-Cultural Research on Organizational Leadership: A Critical Analysis and a Proposed Theory." In *New Perspectives in International Industrial Organizational Psychology*, eds. P.C. Earley and M. Erez, 535–625. San Francisco: New Lexington, This work also includes a detailed examination of various empirical cross-cultural leadership studies.

[2] House, R.J., P. Hanges, S. Ruiz-Quintanilla, P. Dorfman, M. Javidan, and M. Dickson. 1999. "Cultural Influences on Leadership and Organizations." *Advances in Global Leadership*, 171–233, 1 Vol. Greenwich, CT: JAI Press, Inc.

[3] Id.

1. Societal culture, in the form of values and practices, affects leader attributes and behaviors (i.e., "what leaders do") in that culture. The GLOBE researchers noted that substantial empirical evidence supports this proposition and that the impact of societal culture can be seen from the very beginning of any organization when the founders, as the original leaders of the organization, borrow from the societal culture they are immersed in to adopt leader behavior patterns that are favored in that culture. The process continues as the founders make a lasting imprint on the behavior of subordinate leaders and subsequent leaders through the use of selective management selection criteria, role modeling, and socialization.

2. The leadership attributes and behaviors of the founders affect organizational form, culture, and practices. As previously noted, the organizational founders establish the initial culture of their organizations and then continue to influence the organizational culture on their own and through the attributes and behaviors that they transfer to the subsequent leaders of the organization that they select, train, and mentor.[4]

3. In addition to the strong influence of the founders and other organizational leaders described earlier, organizational culture is also

---

[4] Substantial empirical research has been conducted regarding the proposition that the initial organizational culture is established by the organizational founders. See, e.g., Schein, E. 1992. *Organizational Culture and Leadership: A Dynamic View*, 2nd ed. San Francisco: Jossey-Bass; Schneider, B. 1987. "The People Make the Place." *Personnel Psychology* 40, no. 3, pp. 437–54; and Schneider, B., H.W. Goldstein, and D.B. Smith. 1995. "The ASA Framework: An Update." *Personnel Psychology* 48, no. 4, pp. 747–83. Similarly, a number of researchers have investigated the ongoing influence of the founders and their chosen subsequent leaders on organizational culture. See, e.g., Thompson, K., and F. Luthans. 1990. "Organizational Culture: A Behavioral Perspective." In *Organizational Climate and Culture*, ed. B. Schneider, 319–44. San Francisco: Jossey-Bass; Yukl, G. 1994. *Leadership in Organizations*, 3rd ed. Englewood Cliffs, NJ: Prentice-Hall; Bass, B.M. 1985. *Leadership and Performance beyond Expectations*, New York, NY: Free Press; Miller, D., and C. Droge. 1986. "Psychological and Traditional Determinants of Structure." *Administrative Science Quarterly* 31, no. 4, pp. 539–60; and Schein, E. 1992. *Organizational Culture and Leadership: A Dynamic View*, 2nd ed. San Francisco: Jossey-Bass.

affected by the values and practices imbedded in the societal culture since the societal culture determines the common implicit leadership and organizational theories held by members of the culture and those members come to expect that their organizational leaders will design an organizational culture that is consistent with the implicit theories dictated by the societal culture.[5]

4. Organizational form, culture, and practices also affect the behaviors of the organizational leaders (i.e., the founders and subsequent leaders) who must respond to the organizational culture and alter their behaviors and leadership styles to align with the implicit leadership and organizational theories held by the organizational members based on their societal culture.[6]

5. As time goes by societal and organizational cultures work together to influence the process by which members of the society and the organizations therein develop shared implicit leadership and organizational theories that are unique to the societal culture (i.e., the "culturally endorsed leadership theories" or "CLTs") and that differentiate it from other societal cultures.[7]

6. While societal culture and leader attributes and behaviors are clearly important influences on organizational culture it is also apparent that organizational culture, and the behaviors and actions of organizational leaders, is affected by strategic organizational contingencies (i.e., size, technology, and environment) that impose requirements that organizations must meet in order to perform effectively, compete, and survive.

7. Organizational form and practices are largely directed toward meeting the requirements imposed on organizations by their specific

[5] See, e.g., Lord, R.G., and K.J. Maher. 1991. *Leadership and Information Processing: Linking Perceptions and Performance.* Boston: Unwin-Everyman.

[6] See, e.g., Schein, E. 1992. *Organizational Culture and Leadership: A Dynamic View*, 2nd ed. San Francisco: Jossey-Bass; and Trice, H.M., and J.M. Beyer. 1984. *The Cultures of Work Organizations.* Englewood Cliffs, NJ: Prentice-Hall.

[7] See, e.g., Lord, R.G., and K.J. Maher. 1991. *Leadership and Information Processing: Linking Perceptions and Performance.* Boston: Unwin-Everyman.

strategic organizational contingencies.[8] However, the relationship between the choices made with regard to organizational form and practices and the strategic organizational contingencies will be moderated by cultural forces. For example, in low uncertainty avoidance cultures it can be expected that forces toward formalization will be weaker and that organizations in those cultures will tend to shy away from excessive reliance on formal rules and procedures. Similarly, organizations in lower power distance cultures are more likely to use a decentralized organizational structure for decision making and delegate authority to lower levels of what is typically a relatively flat organizational hierarchy.

8. Strategic organizational contingencies also affect leader attributes and behaviors. Leaders are selected and adjust their behaviors to meet the requirements of the strategic organizational contingencies that are confronting the organization.

9. Leader acceptance (i.e., acceptance of the legitimacy and authority of the organization leader) is a function of the interaction between the CLTs and the attributes and behaviors of the leader. In order for the leader to be accepted his or her attributes and behaviors must be congruent with the CLTs of the organizational members.

10. Leader effectiveness is influenced both by leader acceptance and by how well the leader deals with the applicable strategic organizational contingencies. Leaders who are not accepted will find it more difficult to influence the actions of their subordinates than leaders who are accepted. Leaders who effectively address strategic organizational contingencies will be more effective than leaders who do not.

11. Leader effectiveness influences leader acceptance. Leaders who are effective in addressing the applicable strategic organizational contingencies will, in the long run, be accepted by all or most of his or her subordinates. Those subordinates who do not accept their leaders will eventually leave the organization voluntarily or through dismissal.

---

[8] See, e.g., Burns, T., and G.M. Stalker. 1961. *The Management of Innovation.* London: Tavistock Publications, Tavistock Centre; and Lawrence, P., and J. Lorsch. 1967. *Organization and Environment.* Cambridge, MA: Harvard University Press.

The GLOBE researchers summarized the practical consequences of their implied theory by noting that the attributes and practices that distinguish societal cultures from each other, as well as strategic organizational contingencies confronting the organization, are predictive of the attributes and behaviors of organizational leaders, and organizational practices, that are most frequently perceived as acceptable are most frequently enacted, and are most effective. The theory is presented as a systems model and the GLOBE researchers concede that it is too complex to be tested in its entirety; however, the researchers suggest that the various linkages and relationships described earlier can be rigorously tested and that these tests can be used to infer the validity of the model.

One of the interesting features of the model is the feasibility of incorporating the possibility of cultural change and/or changes in the applicable strategic organizational contingencies. For example, societies may be exposed to new competitive forces—and accumulate new common experiences—as a result of exposure to international media, cross-border commerce, international political and economic competition, and other forms of interaction with other societal cultures and this may eventually lead to changes in the societal culture and/or the prevalent CLTs. Strategic organizational contingencies are also likely to change as time goes by as a result of changes in the economic or political environment or the emergence of new technologies. Leaders may respond to these changes by adopting new behaviors and/or implementing new organizational practices that initially clash with established cultural norms yet that are necessary in order for the organization to effectively meet the changing requirements of the strategic organizational contingencies. Resistance to new leadership and organizational practices that are inconsistent with the existing CLTs can be expected and has been confirmed in various research studies.[9] However, the GLOBE researchers hypothesized that eventually

---

[9] See, e.g., Gagliardi, P. 1986. "The Creation and Change of Organizational Cultures: A Conceptual Framework." *Organization Studies* 7, no. 2, pp. 117–34; and Hanges, P.J., R.G. Lord, D.V. Day, W.P. Sipe, W. Smith, and D.J. Brown. 1997. "Leadership and Gender Bias: Dynamic Measures and Nonlinear Modeling." In *R.G. Lord (Chair), Dynamic systems, leadership perceptions, and gender effects. Symposium presented at the Twelfth Annual Conference of the Society of Industrial and Organizational Psychology.* Not surprisingly, resistance varies among members of

the new leader behaviors and practices, often with modifications to accommodate existing norms, will constitute new shared common experiences among the societal members that will be incorporated into the CLTs that distinguish and define the societal culture.

Zagoršek's Assessment of Culture's Influence on Leadership

Several years after the GLOBE researchers published their "integrated theory," Zagoršek, who was studying the usage of five leadership practices of transformational leadership by MBA students from six countries (Argentina, India, Korea, Nigeria, Slovenia, and the United States),[10] provided an interesting and comprehensive list and explanation of ways in which culture can influence leadership styles and behaviors:

Culture plays an important role in shaping the approved leadership prototype—the image of the ideal leader—of a particular society. The leadership prototype includes, among other things, a list of the leader attributes or behaviors that are presumed to be desirable and necessary in order for a leader to be effective and accepted by his or her subordinates.[11]

Culture has a significant—many say fundamental—influence on the personality traits and work values of leaders and their subordinates in a particular society. It has been suggested that personality is the end result of a lifelong process of interaction between an individual and his or her

---

the organization based on individual variables (e.g., personality, stereotypical attitudes) and situational factors (e.g., mental workload, job-context). Id.

[10] Zagoršek, H. September 2004. "Assessing the Impact of National Culture on Leadership: A Six Nation Study." https://researchgate.net/publication/320274490_Leadership_A_Global_Survey_of_Theory_and_Research

[11] See M.S. O'Connell, R. Lord, and M.K. O'Connell. 1990. "Differences in Japanese and American Leadership Prototypes: Implications for Cross-Cultural Training." Paper presented at the Academy of Management, San Francisco; House, R. 1998. "A Brief History of GLOBE." *Journal of Managerial Psychology* 13, nos. 3/4, pp. 230–41; and R. House, P. Hanges, A. Ruiz-Quintanilla, P. Dorfman, M. Javidan, M. Dickson et al. 1999. "Cultural Influences in Leadership and Organizations: Project GLOBE." In *Advances in Global Leadership*, eds. W. Mobley, M. Gessner and V. Arnold, 171–233, 1 Vol. Stamford, CT: JAI Press.

eco-cultural and socio-cultural environment and these environmental influences, which differ from culture to culture, will inevitably lead to identifiable systematic differences in the personality traits of individuals that grow up in different cultural societies.[12]

The cultural values and norms of a society determine the attitudes of leaders and their actual pattern of leadership behaviors. Among other things, cultural values define societal norms regarding the ways in which members of the society, including leaders and their subordinates, relate to one another and these norms specify acceptable forms of leadership behaviors. In some cases, norms relating to leadership behaviors will actually be formalized in the form of laws that leaders must adhere to as they exercise their powers to influence the actions of their subordinates.[13]

Just as cultural values and norms impact the attitudes and behaviors of leaders, they also influence how subordinates perceive and ultimately accept or reject the behaviors and practices of their leaders. Zagoršek noted that research has confirmed that "[f]ollowers across nations differ in their preferences for, acceptance of, and performance responses to different communication patterns, task- versus person-orientation, close versus general supervision, democratic versus autocratic leadership, and usage of participatory practices.[14]"

Consistent with the points previously discussed, culture is an important determinant of the effectiveness of particular leadership styles and behaviors and leader behaviors that are inconsistent with societal norms and values and/or with the implicit leadership theories of subordinates in the society are likely to be ineffective and ultimately lower the morale of the subordinates and harm the productivity and performance of the organizational unit that the ineffective leader oversees.

---

[12] Berry, J.W., Y.H. Poortinga, M.H. Segall, and P.R. Dasen. 2002. *Cross-Cultural Psychology: Research and Applications*, 2nd ed. Cambridge: Cambridge University Press.

[13] Yukl, G. 2002. *Leadership in Organizations*, 5th ed. Upper Saddle River, NJ: Prentice Hall.

[14] House, R.J., N.S. Wright, and R. Aditya. 1997. "Cross-Cultural Research on Organizational Leadership: A Critical Analysis and a Proposed Theory." In *New Perspectives in International Industrial Organizational Psychology*, eds. P. Earley and M. Erez, 535–625. San Francisco: New Lexington.

Culture is important in providing leaders with guidance regarding the outcomes and results that they should try to achieve through their decisions, actions, and behaviors. Leaders must understand the desired goals and objectives of their subordinates and realize that there are differences among societies in this regard. For example, subordinates in India appear to value job satisfaction more than productivity, British workers are most interested in self-actualization, and the French seek good working relations and security.[15]

Culture impacts how leaders are selected and accepted as "legitimate" within societies. As Zagoršek explained

> ...in Egalitarian, Individualistic, low Power Distance societies the leader usually has to "earn his title"—he or she is "appointed" by the followers, who admire his or her qualities and achievements. In more traditional, Collectivistic, and high Power Distance countries, the leadership role is usually ascribed to an individual by the nature of his or her status (acquired by birth, kinship, gender, age, education, or connections).

Research has also identified other factors that are generally more important than others in particular societies in influencing how leaders are selected in those societies including education, class, occupation, ownership, and technical expertise and presumably these preferences are determined to some degree by the society's cultural environment.[16]

---

[15] Sinha, D. 1984. "Psychology in the Context of the Third World Development." *International Journal of Psychology* 19, nos. (1–4), pp. 17–29 (India); and Kanungo, R., and R. Wright. 1983. "A Cross-Cultural Comparative Study of Managerial Job Attitudes." *Journal of International Business Studies* 14, no. 2, pp. 115–29 (covering Canada, France, Japan and Great Britain).

[16] House, R.J., N.S. Wright, and R.N. Aditya. 1997. "Cross-Cultural Research on Organizational Leadership: A Critical Analysis and a Proposed Theory." In *New Perspectives in International Industrial Organizational Psychology*, eds. P. Earley and M. Erez, 535–625, San Francisco: New Lexington; Boyd, D.P. 1974. "Research Note: The Educational Background of a Selected Group of England's Leaders." *Sociology* 8, no. 2, pp. 305–12; McClelland, D. 1961. *The Achieving Society*. New York, NY: Van Nostrand Reinhold; Lee, S.M., and G. Schwendiman. 1982. *Japanese Management: Cultural and Environmental Considerations*. New York, NY: Praeger.

Differences among societies have been identified with respect to the bases of power and influence tactics that leaders rely upon in order to be effective. In the United States, for example, subordinate effectiveness was found to be positively correlated with supervisor use of referent power while in Bulgaria subordinate effectiveness was positively related to the use of legitimate power by supervisors.[17]

The nature of the relationship between leaders and their subordinates is also impacted by cultural factors. In some societies, for example, the relationship is akin to a parent and child and the subordinate is dependent on the leader and the leader is expected to attend to and satisfy the needs of his or her subordinate. In more egalitarian societies, however, there are far fewer distinctions between leaders and subordinates and the leader is often simply "first among equals."

Culture provides context for the styles and behaviors of leaders and thus provides a way to identify whether a particular action will be considered appropriate or inappropriate within a society. For example, in Southeast Asia attendance by a leader at a subordinate's family celebration will be considered "supportive" as will a leader's discussion of the personal problems of one subordinate with other subordinates in Japan; however, such behaviors by a leader in the United States would likely be considered annoying or offensive by the subordinate whose personal space has been intruded upon by the leader.

Culture provides a basis for identifying and defining what Zagoršek referred to as "emic conceptions of leadership" in a society (i.e., how the concept of leadership is perceived in the society). Good leaders understand what subordinates in their society expect of them and seek to behave in ways that are consistent with those expectations. Zagoršek cited the work of Sinha on the "nurturant-task leader" of India, which Sinha described as someone who "understands the expectations of his subordinates. He knows that they relish dependency and personalized relationship, accept his authority and look toward him for guidance and direction."[18]

---

[17] Rahim, M.A., D. Antonioni, K. Krumov, and S. Ilieva. 2010. "Power, Conflict, and Effectiveness: A Cross-Cultural Study in the United States and Bulgaria." *European Psychologist* 5, no. 1, pp. 28–33.

[18] Sinha, J.B.P. 1980. *The Nurturant Task Leader*. New Delhi: Concept Publishing House.

Zagoršek conceded that support for the general proposition that culture does influence the styles and behaviors of leaders comes from a number of studies that have examined behaviors and attitudes of managers in different countries and the effectiveness of various leadership styles in different cultural environments. Referring to the GLOBE researchers, Zagoršek noted that they had identified

[d]ifferences in modal patterns of leadership behaviors across cultures ... with respect to individualistic versus team-orientation, particularism versus universalism, performance—versus maintenance-orientation, paternalism, reliance on personal abilities, subordinates or rules, leader influence processes, decision-making, and service orientation.[19]

Another researcher found that managers from Japan spent more time on single tasks than managers from the United States.[20] A study of managers from Korea, Mexico, Taiwan, and the United States identified clear differences among those countries with respect to the use and effectiveness of the participative leadership style and the degree to which managers shared and controlled information, sought and accepted input from subordinates on decisions, and established and maintained power distance in their relationships with their subordinates.[21] A number of researchers

---

[19] Zagoršek, H. September 2004. "Assessing the Impact of National Culture on Leadership: A Six Nation Study." https://researchgate.net/publication/320274490_Leadership_A_Global_Survey_of_Theory_and_Research (citing House, R.J., N.S. Wright, and R.N. Aditya. 1997. "Cross-Cultural Research on Organizational Leadership: A Critical Analysis and a Proposed Theory." In *New Perspectives in International Industrial Organizational Psychology*, eds. P. Earley and M. Erez, 535–625. San Francisco: New Lexington).

[20] Doktor, R. 1983. "Culture and Management of Time: A Comparison of Japanese and American Top Management Top Practice." *Asia Pacific Journal of Management* 1, no. 1, pp. 65–70.

[21] Dorfman, P.W., and J. Howell. 1997. "Leadership in Western and Asian Countries: Commonalities and Differences in Effective Leadership Processes across Cultures." *Leadership Quarterly* 8, no. 3, pp. 233–75 (participative leadership was much more prevalent among US managers than among managers from the other countries; Taiwanese managers used authoritarian decision styles,

have identified societal differences with respect to the use and effectiveness of transformational, charismatic, inspirational, and visionary leadership styles and behaviors.[22] In addition, several studies have concluded that coercive, directive, and autocratic leadership styles are more commonly found in high power distance countries and that top managers in those countries are more likely to rely upon formal rules and procedures to direct day-to-day activities and are less likely than their colleagues in low power distance countries to seek input from subordinates on how to deal with day-to-day events.[23] Finally, one study found differences among executives from different cultural backgrounds with respect to openness to change in leadership profiles.[24]

---

maintained power distance and tightly controlled information; and participative leadership was ineffective in Mexico due to high collectiveness, low levels of trust and the absence of organizational and relational structures that would facilitate and support participation).

[22] See, e.g., Kouzes, J.M., and B.Z. Posner. 2002. "The Leadership Practices Inventory: The Theory and Evidence Behind the Five Practices of Exemplary Leaders." http://media.wiley.com/assets/61/06/lc_jb_appendix.pdf (accessed December 31, 2018) (visionary, experimenting and supportive behaviors, all typically associated with transformational leadership practices, were used more frequently by US managers than by managers from Switzerland); Kuchinke, K. 1999. "Leadership and Culture: Work-Related Values and Leadership Styles among One Company's U.S. and German Telecommunication Employees." *Human Resource Development Quarterly*. (US managers and employees scored significantly higher than their German counterparts in the same global telecommunications company on charisma and inspirational motivation scales.)

[23] Bass, B.M. 1990. *Bass & Stogdill's Handbook of Leadership: Theory, Research, and Managerial Applications*, 3rd ed. New York, NY: Free Press; Hofstede, G. 1991. *Cultures and Organizations: Software of the Mind*. London; New York, NY: McGraw-Hill; Dickson, M.W., D.N. Den Hartog, and J.K. Mitchelson, "Research on Leadership in a Cross-Cultural Context: Making Progress, and Raising New Questions." *Leadership Quarterly* 14, no. 6, pp. 729–69; and Smith, P.B., M.F. Peterson, and S.H. Schwartz. 2002. "Cultural Values, Sources of Guidance, and Their Relevance to Managerial Behavior - a 47 Nation Study." *Journal of Cross-Cultural Psychology* 33, no. 2, pp. 188–208.

[24] Ekvall, G., and J. Arvonen. 1991. "Change-Centered Leadership: An Extent Ion of the Two-Dimensional Model." *Scandinavian Journal of Management* 7, pp. 17–26. (also finding that culture had a stronger influence on leadership profiles of executives than their professional experience)

While concluding that culture did have an impact on leadership styles and practices, Zagoršek argued that it was important to note that the results of multifactor analyses of data collected in numerous surveys showed that the relative strength of the influence of culture on leadership is small and that, in general, culture at the country levels does not explain that much of the variation in the usage of leadership practices found to occur in different countries.[25] Zagoršek suggested that there were a number of other important variables aside from culture that contribute to the leadership process and its outcomes including, for example,

[c]haracteristics of the leader (personality, capabilities, intelligence, motives, values, and beliefs of leaders), characteristics of followers (their personalities, needs and expectations, skills and expertise, task commitment and effort, and attributions about the

---

[25] Zagoršek, H. September 2004. "Assessing the Impact of National Culture on Leadership: A Six Nation Study." https://researchgate.net/publication/320274490_Leadership_A_Global_Survey_of_Theory_and_Research Zagoršek reported that Haire et al. found that 28% of the questionnaire response variance in their study of managers' need hierarchies in different countries could be accounted for by nationality (culture) and that 52% of the variance in managers' attitudes in a multi-country study conducted by Griffeth et al. could be accounted for by nationality. See Haire, M., E. Ghiselli, and L. Porter. 1966. *Managerial Thinking: An International Study.* New York, NY: Wiley; and Griffeth, R.W., P.W. Hom, A. Denisi, and W. Kirchner. August 1980. "A Multivariate, Multinational Comparison of Managerial Attitudes." Paper presented at the annual meeting of the Academy of Management, Detroit. However, in his own study Zagoršek found that, in general, culture explained between 3% to 8% of the variation in the usage of leadership practices and the GLOBE researchers found that cultural values on both societal and organizational level accounted mostly for between 7% and 27% of the total organizational variance for the four culturally endorsed GLOBE leadership styles. See House, R.J., P. Hanges, A. Ruiz-Quintanilla, P. Dorfman, M. Javidan, M. Dickson et al. 1999. "Cultural Influences in Leadership and Organizations: Project GLOBE." In *Advances in Global Leadership,* 1 Vol. eds. W. Mobley, M. Gessner and V. Arnold, 171–233. Stamford, Connecticut: JAI Press. Zagoršek noted that these results appeared to indicate that cultural variation in organizational leadership styles and behaviors may be much smaller than variation in managerial attitudes or values, which were the focus of the studies conducted by Haire et al. and Griffeth et al.

leader), and characteristics of the situation (type of organization, structure and type of work unit, task structure and complexity, environmental uncertainty, and organizational and national culture).[26]

However, while the direct influence of culture on leadership styles appears to be relatively small, perhaps less than expected by some, it does appear to have a much higher explanatory value with respect to variation than other variables such as gender, age, or work experience and, of course, culture also comes into play indirectly to the extent that it may impact other variables such as the values of leaders and/or the expectations and norms of followers.

Ardichvili and Kuchinke

Ardichvili and Kuchinke, who studied the relationship between cultural dimensions and leadership styles in four former countries of the Soviet Union (Georgia, Kazakhstan, Kyrgyzstan, and Russia), found that while the cultural dimensions that they used predicted leadership styles they accounted for only a small portion of the variance and they suggested that this might mean that "other factors could have stronger effects on leadership than the socio-cultural dimensions."[27] Ardichvili and Kuchinke also noted the possibility that by relying on Hofstede's five-dimensional model they may not have included the "whole universe of socio-cultural dimensions relevant to leadership" and pointed out that the use of models suggested by other researchers that break out dimensions such as individualism-collectivism into multiple components might unearth more

[26] Zagoršek, H. September 2004. "Assessing the Impact of National Culture on Leadership: A Six Nation Study." https://researchgate.net/publication/320274490_Leadership_A_Global_Survey_of_Theory_and_Research

[27] Ardichvili, A., and K. Kuchinke, "Leadership Styles and Cultural Values Among Managers and Subordinates: a Comparative Study of Four Countries of the Former Soviet Union, Germany and the US." *Human Resource Development International* 5, no. 1, pp. 99–117, 113.

information.[28] Ardichvili and Kuchinke have suggested that in light of evidence that the relationship between societal culture and leadership styles may not be that strong further work should be done to investigate the influence of culture on leadership at other levels such as organizational, industry, and professional cultures.[29]

Muczyk and Holt

Muczyk and Holt made several general, and tentative, recommendations regarding the most effective leadership styles for various regions around the world based on the predominant cultural characteristics in those regions identified by various researchers.[30] They began with "mainstream leadership

---

[28] Id. Ardichvili and Kuchinke noted that Triandis had proposed that individualism and collectivism are unique constructs that needed to be split into separate continua as opposed to the approach taken by Hofstede, who viewed individualism and collectivism as poles of a single continuum; and that Triandis had also suggested that both individualism and collectivism may be multifaceted dimensions consisting of more than one component. See, e.g., Triandis, H. 1995. *Individualism and Collectivism*. Boulder, CO: Westview.

[29] Ardichvili, A., and K.P. Kuchinke. 2002. "Leadership Styles and Cultural Values Among Managers and Subordinates: A comparative Study of Four Countries of the Former Soviet Union, Germany and the US." *Human Resource Development International* 5, no. 1, pp. 99–117, 113–14.

[30] Muczyk, J.P., and D.T. Holt. May 2008. "Toward a Cultural Contingency Model of Leadership." *Journal of Leadership & Organizational Studies* 14, no. 4, pp. 277–86, 283. (Table 5: Examples of Regional Leadership Styles Based on Regional Cultural Determinants). Muczyk and Holt argued that "[t]here is considerable support for a global leadership contingency model" and noted that their recommendations were inspired by the work of several researchers, including results and interpretations reported in Brodbeck, F.C., M. Frese, S. Akerblom, G. Audia, G. Bakacsi and H. Bendova, and P. Castel. 2000. "Cultural Variation of Leadership Prototypes Across 22 European Countries." *Journal of Occupational and Organizational Psychology* 73, no. 1, pp. 1–29; Javidan, M. P.W. Dorfman, M.S. de Luque, and R.J. House. February 2006. "In the Eye of the Beholder: Cross cultural Lessons in Leadership from Project GLOBE." *Academy of Management Perspectives* 20, no. 1, pp. 67–90; Koopman, P.L., D.N. Den Hartog, and E. Konrad. 1999. "National Culture and Leadership Profiles in Europe: Some Results from the GLOBE Study." *European Journal of Work and Organizational Psychology* 8, no. 4, 503–20; Laurent, A. 1983. "The Cultural Diversity of

constructs developed from North American experiences" and integrated them with research on cultural imperatives completed using a wide and robust array of multinational samples.[31] They noted that the volume of research threatened to create a global contingency model that might well be far too complex and difficult to be of any practical use to practitioners (i.e., organizational leaders and managers) and sought to create a "simplified version" that could be readily applied.[32] They also cautioned that not all leadership characteristics were a function of cultural factors and that other things, such as attributes of subordinates and requirements of the particular situation, needed to be taken into account when identifying the most appropriate and potentially effective leadership behavior.[33] Finally, like others, Muczyk and Holt questioned whether it was realistic to expect that leaders could be flexible enough to modify their styles whenever cultural conditions dictated the need for a change and suggested that organizations might be better off taking the styles of their leaders as "givens" and then investing their time and effort into placing them into cultural situations where those styles would be appreciated and effective, thus taking advantage of the pre-existing "strengths" of their leaders.[34] Their recommendations for specific geographic regions can be summarized as follows:

- *US and Canada*: With regard to the United States and
  Canada, Muczyk and Holt suggested that the Muczyk/
  Reimann model would be applicable in selecting the leadership style that should be used in particular circumstances.

Western Conceptions of Management." *International Studies of Management and Organizations* 13, nos. (1–2), pp. 75-96; and Ronen, S., and O. Shenkar. July 1985. "Clustering Countries on Attitudinal Dimensions: A Review and Synthesis." *Academy of Management Review* 10, no. 3, p. 449. Muczyk and Holt also cautioned that there are obviously cultural differences within the "country clusters" and that it is necessary and recommended to match the leadership characteristics used in their model to the "specific cultural imperatives" of each country.

[31] Muczyk, J.P., and D. Holt. May 2008. "Toward a Cultural Contingency Model of Leadership." *Journal of Leadership & Organizational Studies* 14, no. 4, pp. 277–86, 278.

[32] Id. at 284.

[33] Id.

[34] Id.

- *Middle East*: Muczyk and Holt suggested that the autocratic leadership style was generally recommended in the Middle East combined with "heavy doses of concern for production and consideration." They noted that "[i]n the Middle East, with the exception of Israel, there are no democratic traditions" and that "the touchstone of good leadership in that part of the world seems to have revolved around the concept of justice, not democracy."[35] As far as rewards are concerned, Middle Eastern cultures are probably more receptive to recognition based on group and organizational performance measures rather than on individual performance. Muczyk and Holt also commented that leaders should include family members of subordinates in organizational social functions in the Middle East.
- *Asia (excluding Japan)*: According to Muczyk and Holt, the preferred leadership style in Asia, other than in Japan, would be "autocratic with an emphasis on consideration."[36] In light of the collectivist nature of these societies, it is not surprising that group and/or organizational measures of performance are recommended as the basis for rewards.
- *Japan*: Most researchers who have worked to identify "country clusters" based on cultural dimensions have concluded that Japan, although planted firmly in the middle of the Asian geographic zone, should be treated differently

---

[35] Id. at 283. They noted, for example, the absence of democratic traditions in China, including in the workplace. Even in countries that had been exposed to democratic institutions, such as India, the efficacy of Western leadership styles might be problematic given that democracy was not introduced to the workplace in those countries. Id. at 278.

[36] Id. at 283. They noted that the region had a history of autocratic rule and that "[a]n autocrat ruled so long as he was on good behavior … [i]n other words, if he treated his subjects in an evenhanded way, honored their traditions, did not publicly flout the Koran, and did not levy onerous taxes, he was expected to rule for life." Id.

than other countries in Asia.[37] Muczyk and Holt recommended that rather than the "autocratic" style preferred elsewhere in Asia, leaders in Japan should apply "democratic leadership … with emphasis on consideration." Interestingly, Muczyk and Holt questioned whether there was any need to tie rewards to performance since workers in Japan appeared to be conditioned to "do the right things because they are right not because of the rewards associated with correct behavior."

- *Western Europe*: For those countries in Western Europe with cultural characteristics similar to those found in the United States and Canada, Muczyk and Holt recommended that the leadership style should be determined based on the Muczyk/Reimann model. However, there are some Western European countries that have a relatively higher regard for hierarchy and "chain of command" and Muczyk and Holt prescribed a leadership style for these countries that was more autocratic.

- *Eastern Europe*: While many countries in Eastern Europe are trying to create economic systems similar to those found in Western Europe, recent history is still hard to overcome and Muczyk and Holt recommended that for the time being it may still make sense to use and autocratic leadership style coupled with concern for production. As for reward systems, individual performance measures may be used.

- *Southern Europe*: Muczyk and Holt recommended autocratic leadership in Southern European countries combined with a heavy emphasis on consideration and reward systems based on group or organizational measures of performance.

---

[37] A number of explanations have been advanced for Japan's apparent differences from the rest of Asia, including its geographic isolation—a group of islands disconnected from the rest of Asia; its long period of diplomatic isolation from other countries, not just in Asia but all around the world; and its language, which is only spoken in Japan. Japan is also unique among countries in Asia because of its intense exposure to U.S. institutions and values after the end of World War II, a factor that likely contributes to the heightened interest and acceptance of "democracy" in Japan in comparison to many of its Asian neighbors.

- *Central and South America*: Muczyk and Holt recommended autocratic leadership with emphasis on concern
  for production in Central and South American countries;
  however, they cautioned that leaders should not ignore the
  need for consideration in these countries. Reward systems in
  Central and South America would best when they are based
  on group or organizational measures of performance.

Hofstede on Cross-Cultural Transfer of U.S. Leadership Theories

A good deal of the research activities conducted in the field of comparative management studies seeks to identify and explain similarities and
differences among various management systems. In addition, the field
has included the pursuit of universally, or at least broadly, applicable
management systems, philosophies, values, and practices that can be
transferred effectively across cultures with predictable and desired results.
The transfer is a complex process involving not only the technical aspects
of a particular management system but also verification that the application of the principles associated with that system is having the desired
behavioral impact in the specific cultural and environmental context in
which the transfer is occurring.

Long before the GLOBE researchers embarked on their comprehensive analysis and assessment of the influence of culture on leadership,
Hofstede had put forth a number of arguments regarding attempts to
transfer U.S. leadership theories to other countries. In fact, one of the
primary objectives that Hofstede had when first publishing his research
results was to demonstrate how the cultural environment identified in a
particular country influenced the theories of leadership and management
practices that were developed and used in those countries. His view was
quite clear on this matter—theories of leadership and management reflect
the cultural environment in which they were written—and Hofstede
believed this was not only true of theories produced in the United States,
by far the largest producer and attempted exporter of management theories in the world, but also of ideas developed in centuries past by Old
World philosophers living and writing in ancient Greece (Plato), medieval

and Renaissance England (More), Italy (Machiavelli), France (Fayol), and Germany (Weber) during the early 20th Century.[38] Hofstede also noted that the views of leadership and management theorists reflect their own economic and educational background, as well as national factors, and that it was therefore not surprising to him that most modern theories of leadership and management reflected a "national intellectual middle-class culture background" since management pundits tend to be "middle-class intellectuals."[39]

Assuming for the moment that Hofstede is correct about the strong impact that a theorist's cultural background has on his or her theories of leadership and management the next question, which was posed by Hofstede himself, is "[t]o what extent do theories developed in one country and reflecting the cultural boundaries of that country apply to other countries"?[40] Theorists seeking, and believing in, universal leadership or management principles implicitly took the position that their theories could be applied in every country regardless of the cultural dimensions that dominate in that country. However, is it really true that U.S. theories of leadership and management can be effectively applied in India, Japan, or poor developing countries? Hofstede argued that at the time of his survey little work had been done on this question and that the cultural dimensions that he had identified provided the tools necessary to analyze whether well-known U.S. theories of leadership, motivation, and organization could be readily applied in other countries with different cultural dimensions.

Hofstede argued that the theories regarding leadership that are developed and used in a particular country are determined by the cultural values of that country, particularly the position of that country on the power distance axis. He first illustrated this idea by looking back in history to the well-known, yet often criticized, management techniques espoused by Machiavelli in Italy in the late 15th and early 16th centuries and pointing out that the Machiavellian practices of deceit, bribery, manipulation, and

---

[38] Hofstede, G. 1980. "Motivation, Leadership and Organization: Do American Theories Apply Abroad?" *Organization Dynamics* 9, no. 1, pp. 42–63, 49–50.
[39] Id. at 50.
[40] Id.

murder were consistent with the then-current Italian society in which power distances were quite large. Hofstede contrasted Machiavelli to the contemporaneous writings of Sir Thomas More in England whose call for consensus in *Utopia* was to be expected given the lower power distance in the cultural environment in which he lived and taught. Interestingly, the success of both Machiavelli and More in their own time depended largely on political considerations—Machiavelli was able to survive through cunning and pragmatism while More lost his life because his ideas were perceived as too threatening and critical by those in power over the country.[41]

Hofstede then turned to several popular leadership theories that have been developed in the United States, and which were being packaged and promoted as possible solutions for managers operating in other countries, including McGregor's Theory X and Theory Y, Likert's System Four management model, and Blake and Mouton's Grid Theory. Hofstede grouped all of these theories into what he referred to as the "participative management" school since the common thread among them was a recommendation that subordinates be afforded opportunities to participate in the management decisions made by their leaders; however, the onus was on the leader/manager to initiate this process as part of his/her leadership style. Hofstede explained that these forms of participative management theories could be expected from a society such as the United States given its middle position on the power distance axis (15th out of the 40 countries in the survey) but that such theories would likely not be comfortable in countries appearing at other points on the axis. For example, large power distance countries, such as France and Italy, that perhaps not fully embracing the draconian principles of Machiavelli would nonetheless have little interest in the type of subordinate participation in management advocated in the United States. On the other end of the spectrum, however, countries with smaller power distances than the United States (e.g., Germany, Israel, Norway, and Sweden) would not only endorse participative management but would incorporate mechanisms for subordinate initiation, referred to as "industrial democracy," that were not popular in the United States and often resisted by industrial leaders. Interestingly, the

---

[41] Id. at 56.

position of small power distance countries on the uncertainty avoidance axis appeared to impact how they implemented industrial democracy—weak uncertainty avoidance countries like Sweden, more risk tolerant, relied on small and informal initiatives at the local level before formalizing matters in the form of legislation; and strong uncertainty avoidance countries like Germany that are used to relying on extensive sets of written rules and regulations would pass laws first and then work to have them implemented on a day-to-day basis at the organizational level.[42]

Hofstede did astutely point out that managers cannot simply choose the style of leadership that they prefer to use and expect that it will be accepted and appreciated by subordinates and he criticized management theorists as being naïve if they thought that effective leadership was simply up to the preferences and talents of the manager. Hofstede noted that the measures of power distance generated from this survey were based on the values of people as subordinates and not on the values of their leaders and this was important since the cultural conditioning of the subordinates determined how they would react to the leadership styles of their managers.[43] He then described some of the key attributes of "subordinateship" that he believed could generally be found in countries at different levels of power distance. For example, in countries, such as the United States, where the level of power distance could be categorized as "medium," Hofstede argued that subordinates have medium dependence needs generally and medium dependence needs toward their superiors and that the following is also typically true: subordinates expect superiors to consult with them but will accept autocratic behavior as well; the ideal type of superior for most people is a resourceful democrat; laws and rules apply to everyone but a certain level of privileges for superiors is considered to be normal; and status symbols for superiors contribute moderately to their authority and will be accepted by subordinates.[44]

Hofstede specifically criticized McGregor, Likert, and Blake and Mouton for failing to take into account the cultural profile of the

---

[42] Hofstede, G. 1980. "Motivation, Leadership and Organization: Do American Theories Apply Abroad." *Organization Dynamics* 9, no. 1, pp. 42–63, 56–57.

[43] Id. at 57.

[44] Id. at 61.

subordinates who are expected to respond to the styles and behaviors of their leaders and argued that their prescriptions for how organizational leaders should act would have limited effectiveness outside of the United States and those other countries, such as Australia, Canada, Denmark, Israel, or New Zealand, where the power distance level fell into the small or medium category.[45] He suggested that U.S. managers asked to serve in countries with different power distances would need to learn how to adapt their managerial styles to suit the particular environment in which they were operating and the typical expectations of subordinates in that environment regarding the authority and status of their leaders and the degree to which subordinates participate in the managerial decision-making processes.

Hofstede first considered the difficulties that U.S. managers might face in countries, such as Hong Kong, Indonesia, Mexico, the Philippines, Singapore, and Venezuela[46], where the level of power distance could be categorized as "large." Hofstede claimed that subordinates in these countries have strong dependence needs generally and strong dependence needs toward their superiors and that the following is also typically true:

---

[45] Id. at 57. Power distance was also a predictor of endorsement of the participative leadership style in the GLOBE country clusters and the GLOBE researchers found that the participative leadership style was endorsed in those GLOBE country clusters where small power distance was the norm—the Anglo, Germanic Europe and Nordic Europe clusters. See Dorfman, P.W., P.J. Hanges, and F.C. Brodbeck. 2004. "Leadership Prototypes and Cultural Variation: The Identification of Culturally Endorsed Implicit Theories of Leadership." In *Culture, Leadership, and Organizations: The GLOBE Study of 62 Societies*, eds. R. House, P. Hanges, M. Javidan, P. Dorfman and V. Gupta. Thousand Oaks CA: Sage.

[46] Id. at 51. Just as the GLOBE researchers found that participative leadership was endorsed in country clusters where small power distances were more prevalent their results also indicated that the participative leadership style was not embraced as strongly in country clusters whose members had larger power distances scores such as the Confucian Asia, East Europe, Middle Eastern and Southern Asia clusters. See Dorfman, P.W., P.J. Hanges, and F.C. Brodbeck. 2004. "Leadership Prototypes and Cultural Variation: The Identification of Culturally Endorsed Implicit Theories of Leadership." In *Culture, Leadership, and Organizations: The GLOBE Study of 62 Societies*, eds. R. House, P. Hanges, M. Javidan, P. Dorfman and V. Gupta. Thousand Oaks CA: Sage.

subordinates expect superiors to act autocratically; the ideal type of superior for most people is a benevolent autocrat or paternalist; everybody
expects superiors to enjoy privileges and laws and rules differ for superiors
and subordinates; and status symbols are very important and contribute strongly to the superior's authority with the subordinates.[47] Hofstede
explained that in order for U.S. managers, or managers from other small
or medium power distance countries, to be effective in these countries
they needed to learn how to behave in a more autocratic fashion and then
referred to the colonial history in most Western countries as evidence that
this transition generally can be completed.[48]

Things become more difficult for U.S. managers when they move
to countries, such as Austria, Denmark, Germany, Israel, and Sweden,[49]
where the level of power distance could be categorized as "small." Hofstede
claimed that subordinates in these countries have weak dependence needs
generally and weak dependence needs toward their superiors and that the
following is also typically true: subordinates expect superiors to consult
them and may rebel or strike if superiors are not seen as staying within
their legitimate role; the ideal type of superior is a loyal democrat; laws
and rules apply to all and privileges for superiors are not considered to

---

[47] Id. at 61. Adler also examined the same popular US leadership theories
that Hofstede focused on and reached similar conclusions; specifically, that
the participatory management styles widely lauded in the United States would
not be appropriate for high power distance cultures like China and Japan since
employees in those countries prefer and expect leadership to come from their
supervisors and would be uncomfortable with the delegation of discretionary
decision making authority that is a core feature of participatory management. See
Adler, N. 1991. *International Dimensions of Organizational Behavior*, 14–178,
2nd ed. Boston: PWS-Kent Publishing Co.

[48] Id. at 57. Hofstede suggested that subordinates in large power distance countries may be even more comfortable with superiors who are "real autocrats" (i.e.,
they come from countries where the power distance is also large) than with superiors from lower power distance countries who are attempting to act in a manner
that is out of character for them.

[49] Id. Hofstede found the largest power distance indexes in countries such as
Malaysia, China, Hong Kong, Indonesia, the Philippines, and Singapore, in a
number of Arab countries, and in Latin and South American countries such as
Guatemala, Mexico, Panama, and Venezuela. Id. at 51.

be acceptable; and status symbols are frowned upon and will quickly be criticized and attacked by subordinates.[50] The problem for U.S. managers in these countries lies in their ability to understand and accept the notion of "industrial democracy" that has caught on in these countries and that essentially rejects the principle of managerial prerogative, an idea that is fundamental to the way in which U.S. managers think and operate. U.S. managers in small power distance countries must learn to cope with unfamiliar processes that require consultation with subordinates and often allow subordinates, acting collectively in groups, to take the initiative in areas where the managers are used to leading in a directive fashion.[51]

Hofstede also commented on how well one might expect Drucker's well-known "management by objectives" ("MBO") to be accepted in cultural environments other than the United States. In brief, MBO, which was first introduced by Drucker in the 1950s[52] and was much discussed during the time that Hofstede first released his survey results, was based on the principle that individual efforts must be put together to achieve a common goal known to, and accepted by, everyone in the organization and required the completion of the following steps: organizational objectives must be defined at the very top of the hierarchy, such as the board level; management roles and activities should be analyzed so that duties and responsibilities relating to achievement of the objectives can be properly allocated among the individual managers; performance standards should be established; managers and subordinates should agree upon and

---

[50] Id. at 61.

[51] Id. at 57–58. The difficulties associated with understanding and executing leadership styles that are most likely to be effective in a particular cultural environment should not be underestimated. In fact, in a large survey of managers from 20 countries Geletkanycz found that openness to change in strategies and leadership styles varied among managers with different cultural values, a finding that supports the proposition that culture plays a much more important role than professional training and background in influencing the styles and practices of managers. Geletkanycz, M.A. 1997. "The Salience of "Culture's Consequences": The Effects of Cultural Values on Top Executive Commitment to the Status Quo." *Strategic Management Journal* 18, no. 8, pp. 615–34.

[52] Drucker, P. 1954. *The Practice of Management*. New York, NY: Harper & Row.

define specific objectives for the activities of the subordinates; the targets set for each subordinate should be aligned with the larger objectives of the organization; and management information systems should be created to monitor performance and the actual relationship of individual achievement to organizational objectives.

Hofstede argued that, not surprisingly, several of the assumptions underlying MBO could be traced to cultural dimensions that were comfortable for the United States. First of all, MBO, which contemplates a good deal of dialog between organizational units, and managers and subordinates, regarding objectives, targets, and standards, assumes that subordinates have sufficient independence and confidence to engage in meaningful negotiations with persons higher in the organizational hierarchy (i.e., small or medium power distance). Second, MBO assumes that everyone in the organization, subordinates and their managers, is willing to take risks (i.e., weak uncertainty avoidance). Finally, MBO assumes that subordinates and managers all believe that performance, as measured by achievement of organizational goals and related individual targets, is important (i.e., high masculinity). He then discussed how well MBO might be received in countries with a different cultural profile. In Germany, for example, Hofstede noted that its small power distance should support and welcome dialog within the organization regarding goals and objectives but that problems might arise with respect to acceptance of risk given that Germany is a much stronger uncertainty avoidance society.[53] Attempts to implement MBO in France were a failure in Hofstede's view because France is a large power distance society in which

---

[53] Hofstede, G. 1980. "Motivation, Leadership and Organization: Do American Theories Apply Abroad." *Organization Dynamics* 9, no. 1, pp. 42–63, 58. Hofstede does point out that MBO can fit well with German small power distance/strong uncertainty avoidance to the extent that mutually agreed upon objectives provide subordinates with direction that alleviates stress while also removing the threat of arbitrary authority exercised by superiors. Hofstede cites studies of the use of MBO in German-speaking countries that illustrate a preference for the elaborate formal information systems suggested by Drucker and an emphasis on group objectives that is consistent with the low individualism values in these countries. Id.

managers are uncomfortable with decentralizing authority and subordinates do not expect managers to delegate authority and, in fact, prefer that managers provide direction through a hierarchical structure that reduces stress and anxiety by its very predictability.[54]

---

[54] Id. at 58–59. Initially it was thought that MBO might be a means for implementing what some believed was a long overdue democratization of management processes within French organizations; however, the cultural aversion to participatory management practices, shared by persons at all levels of the organizational hierarchy, proved too difficult to overcome in most instances and Hofstede reported that the French version of MBO—referred to as DPPO (Direction Participative par Objectifs)—had largely been discredited by the time that he first published his survey results at the end of the 1970s. Id.

CHAPTER 7

Culture and Leadership in Developing Countries

Introduction

The field of "leadership studies" has long been primarily focused on Western leadership styles and practices. This occurred for various reasons including the location of the critical mass of researchers in the United States and the fact that most companies operated primarily in the United States with some cautious expansion into foreign markets with similar linguistic and cultural traditions. However, several factors—globalization of the workforce, expansion of operations into numerous markets around the world, and exposure to increased global competition—have forced leadership scholars to incorporate culture into their research and theories since leaders of businesses of all sizes in all countries must be prepared to interact with customers and other business partners from different cultures and leaders of larger companies have the additional challenge of managing multinational organizations and aligning a global corporate culture with multiple and diverging national cultures. In addition, there has been a growing recognition that the study of leadership in developing countries, and training of prospective leaders in those countries, is important because leaders in developing countries can, "by creating vision, direction and collective purposes," play a pivotal role in resolving multiple collection action problems that impede social development and economic growth in those countries.[1]

---

[1] de Ver, Leadership, H.L. April 2008. "Politics and Development: A Literature Survey (Development Leadership Program, Background Paper)." 4. www.dlprog. org/ftp/.../Leadership,%20Politics%20and%20Development.pdf (accessed December 31, 2018).

It is now well accepted that leadership "matters" when it comes to economic growth and development, a conclusion that follows the previous realization that institutions are important contributors to the social and economic progress of developing countries. However, scholars such as de Ver have been critical of research efforts relating to leadership in developing countries, arguing that "many of the conceptions of leadership in the literature are Western-oriented, universalist or individualistic, and there are few conceptions which either incorporate a political understanding of leadership as a process or which have developmental salience."[2] She has also expressed a concern that little analysis has been conducted on how leadership can be practiced in what she describes as "the very often unstable, hybrid and evolving institutional contexts which characterize the condition of many developing countries." She counseled that leadership needed to be understood as a political process, particularly in developing countries, and leadership occurred "within a given indigenous configuration of power, authority and legitimacy, shaped by history, institutions, goals and political culture." She noted that in developing countries, leaders must be able to forge formal or informal coalitions, vertical or horizontal, to solve collective action problems and that the influence of informal institutions is much greater in developing countries and it was thus imperative for leaders to understand those institutions and engage with them in order to be effective.

After conducting an extensive survey of the general literature on "leadership," de Ver concluded that relatively little work had been done on leadership in the specific context of developing countries and the unique problems that the social, economic, and political environments in those countries create for their prospective leaders. Her specific findings included the following[3]:

---

[2] de Ver, H.L. March 2009. "Conceptions of Leadership (Development Leadership Program, Background Paper)." www.dlprog.org/ftp/.../Conceptions%20of%20Leadership.pdf (accessed December 31, 2018).

[3] de Ver, Leadership, H.L. April 2008. "Politics and Development: A Literature Survey (Development Leadership Program, Background Paper)." 3–6. www.dlprog.org/ftp/.../Leadership,%20Politics%20and%20Development.pdf (accessed December 31, 2018).

- Leadership as concept and practice has neither been properly researched nor understood analytically as a key element in the politics of economic growth and social development and the available literature seldom addresses those key issues.
- The bulk of the literature focuses on individuals and individual capacities, or attributes (i.e., individual leaders' characteristics, qualities, attributes, or traits), and not on leadership as a political process involving both leaders' relations with followers and, more critically, elites and coalitions and their interactions.
- Much of the general leadership literature has a distinctly Western, business-related focus with a particular emphasis on leadership from a managerial and organizational perspective. This is not surprising given that most of the scholars working in the field of "leadership studies"' are based in the United States and many of the leading textbooks on the subject have generally included few case studies and examples set in the developing world while focusing most of the attention on Western management systems.
- Only a small body of "mainstream leadership literature" addresses the role of leadership for economic and social development and what is available is largely confined to empirical studies of individual cases.
- What literature there is on leadership in developing countries pays little attention to issues concerning leaders, elites, and coalitions.
- There are substantial policy-relevant research gaps to be filled. For example, de Ver urges the research community to move toward creating and expanding a library of case studies that illustrate the role that leaders, elites, and coalitions in developing countries have played in successfully achieving sustained economic growth, social development, and organizational success. Cases studies should focus on national, subnational, sectorial, and organizational activities.

While de Ver's critiques are varied and diverse, she correctly points out the problems that arise when so much of the leadership-related research is based on an assumption of universal acceptance of Western business culture, which she describes as one "in which profit is the main indicator of success and the main goal."[4] The following passage illustrates how and why application of a Western "cultural hegemomy" can lead to puzzling and problematic results in developing countries:

> [In the West there is] the belief that people are rational actors, that markets should be given predominance over the state, and that individualism and competition have inherent merits. In other cultures, however, these assumptions are not universally accepted and often the opposite is the case. For example … in much of East Asia emphasis is placed on conformity, notions of interpersonal harmony and collectivism or group-centeredness. This is in clear contrast to the Western functionalist paradigm where emphasis is placed on autonomy, competition between individuals and groups, performance and self-assertion. In Africa, a different culture of leadership, again, is visible, with emphasis on ceremony, ritual, interpersonal relations, reciprocity, and the distribution of scant resources to clan and ethnic affiliates over and above profit and competition.[5]

Another problem with relying on Western-based notions of organizational and managerial leadership for analyzing developing countries is the implicit assumption that the political environment and business systems are relatively stable. In fact, formal rules, regulations, and accepted practices are often unavailable, or ignored, in developing countries. While the situation is slowly changing as developing countries engage in wholesale restructuring and strengthening of their institutions it is still generally the case that leaders in developing countries must operate in an environment

---

[4] Id.

[5] Id. at 16 (based on omitted quotes from, and citations to Blunt, P., and M.L. Jones. 1997. "Exploring the Limits of Western Leadership Theory in East Asia and Africa." *Personnel Review* 26, nos. (1–2), pp. 6–23).

in which rules change constantly and change is accepted slowly and often with great suspicion by followers. This is one of the reasons that a key role of an organizational leader in a developing country is protecting the organization against the possibility of adverse changes in policy by public institutions, since the state continues to exercise substantial influence in the marketplaces of developing countries.

As in all countries, leaders in developing countries act within a specific sociocultural environment and the characteristics of that environment are presumed to be important determinants of the efficacy of the leader's style and practices. Aycan suggested a profile of the "typical" cultural environment in developing countries that included a strong emphasis on relationships and networking; a strong family orientation that impacts both the personal and work lives of society members; low individual performance orientation, consistent with the strong relationship orientation and collectivist nature of most developing country societies; a low sense of control and self-efficacy, leading to a feeling of "fatalism" and a sense that events are out of the control of society members; downward, indirect, and nonconfrontational communication patterns; and, finally, a strong authority orientation rooted in respect, loyalty, and deference toward those in positions of authority.[6] She also cautioned, however, that there are certain significant cultural differences among the large number of countries still classified as "developing" and that within each country one will find differences among individuals—due to education, socioeconomic status, or age, regional and ethnic subcultures, and business organizations (e.g., subsidiaries of multinational corporations will likely have different cultural orientations than indigenous family-owned businesses).

Using societal culture as a reference point, Pasa et al. provided a suggested list of the expectations and assumptions of leaders in developing countries with respect to their followers along with a profile of leader preferences regarding their own styles and behaviors. Specifically, they argued that in developing countries leaders "are more likely to assume

---

[6] Aycan, Z. 2004. "Leadership and Teamwork in Developing Countries: Challenges and Opportunities." In *Online Readings in Psychology and Culture*, eds. W. Lonner, D. Dinnel, S. Hayes and D. Sattler. http://ac.wwu.edu/~culture/readings.htm

that their employees have an external locus of control, have limited and fixed potential, operate from a time perspective that is past and present oriented and have a short-time focus."[7] With respect to the actual behavior of leaders in developing countries, Pasa et al. predicted that they

> are more likely to encourage a passive or reactive stance to task performance, judge success on moralism derived from tradition and religion, favour an authoritarian or paternalistic orientation and accept that consideration of the context overrides principles and rules.[8]

Jaeger observed that

> [t]he relatively high power distance and the authoritarian/paternalistic people orientation of developing countries imply a certain type of leadership behaviour and leader-follower relationship ... characterized as being more congruent with 'Theory X' leadership, which ... presupposes limited and fixed human potential.

It is certainly problematic and dangerous to make generalizations regarding the elements of societal culture that can be found in the large swath of countries around the world that are classified as "developing." However, cultural profiles developed by researchers may be used as a means for creating hypotheses about the issues and problems that will likely confront leaders in developing countries and the solutions that might be used in order to motivate followers to act in ways that contribute to the achievement of goals established for the organization. In addition, understanding the cultural profile of the country in which a leader is operating provides a clue regarding the preferred personality traits and

---

[7] Fikret Pasa, S., H. Kabasakal, and M. Bodur. 2001. "Society, Organisations and Leadership in Turkey." *Applied Psychology: An International Review* 50, no. 4, pp. 559–89, 563 (citing Kanungo, R.N., and A.M. Jaeger. 1990. "Introduction: The Need for Indigenous Management in Developing Countries." In *Management in Developing Countries*, eds. A. Jaeger and R. Kanungo, London: Routledge).

[8] Id. at 563.

work values of leaders; the manner in which leaders should seek to relate to their subordinates, including the degree to which leaders are expected to be involved in the personal affairs of subordinates and their families; the basis upon which a leader can attain "legitimacy" in the eyes of those that he or she is seeking to leader; and, finally, the effectiveness of particular leadership styles and behaviors.[9]

Relationship Orientation and Paternalism

The strong relationship orientation found in many developing countries explains the popularity and prevalence of the paternalistic leadership style in developing countries. Leaders, like others in those countries, place great importance on establishing and maintaining interpersonal relationships with others including subordinates in the workplace. In turn, subordinates also expect a relationship with their superior that is personal yet professional and characterized by protection, close guidance, and supervision. In exchange for the responsibilities that leaders take for their lives, subordinates are loyal and deferential to their leaders and are generally willing to follow their directions without question or criticism. The paternalistic relationship between leaders and subordinates in developing countries is analogous to a parent-child relationship and, as is the case in the familial context, the relationship is hierarchical with the leader assumed to "know better" for the subordinates in all areas of their lives: personal, professional, and family-related matters.[10]

Aycan argues that the evidence of paternalism can be found in numerous acts by both leaders and subordinates within and outside the workplace. For example, Aycan explains that

---

[9] Jaeger, A.M. 1990. "The Applicability of Western Management Techniques in Developing Countries: A Cultural Perspective." In *Management in Developing Countries*, eds. A. Jaeger and R. Kanungo, London: Routledge, pp. 131–45, 263, 139.

[10] Aycan, Z. 2002. "Leadership and Teamwork in Developing Countries: Challenges and Opportunities." In *Online Readings in Psychology and Culture*, eds. W. Lonner, D. Dinnel, S. Hayes and D. Sattler.

[t]he paternalistic leader gives advice (often times unsolicited) and guides employees in personal, professional (e.g., make career planning on their behalf), and family-related matters (e.g., do marriage counseling, resolve disputes between husband and wives, etc.); shows concern for the well-being of the subordinate as well as his/her family; attends congratulatory (e.g., weddings) and condolence (e.g., funerals) ceremonies of employees as well as their immediate family members; when in need, provides financial assistance to employees (in form of donations or sometimes as loans) in, for example, housing, health care, and educational expenses of their children; allows them to attend personal or family-related problems by letting them leave early or take a day off; acts as a mediator in interpersonal conflicts among employees, and even talks to the disputed party on behalf of the other (without his knowledge or consent) to resolve the conflict.[11]

In return, subordinates are willing to go to great lengths to demonstrate their loyalty and deference to their leaders including

engaging in extra-role behavior or working overtime (unpaid) upon the request of the supervisor; not quitting the job (even if one receives a much better job offer) because of loyalty; following the paternalistic superior to another organization if s/he quits the company; not questioning nor disagreeing with the superior in decisions regarding the company or the employee (e.g., performance evaluations, career-planning, etc.); doing personal favors for the superior when needed (e.g., helping him during the construction of his house); putting extra effort in the job and working hard, so not to lose face to the superior.[12]

Family Orientation

Family orientation is an important influence on societal culture in developing countries and plays an important part in how subordinates view

---

[11] Id.

[12] Id.

work activities in the larger context of their lives and how subordinates expect their leaders to act in an organizational context. In most cases, subordinates view work primarily as a means for satisfying the needs of their families and advancing the family's status within society. In addition, subordinates expect that the organizations they work for will take care of them and their families and it is common to find organizations offering health and educational services to their workers and their families, contributing to housing and heating expenses, and providing financial assistance to workers who may be experiencing problems. Family obligations are routinely allowed to take precedence over work. Aycan explained that "employees feel entitled to absent themselves from work for family-related reasons ... [w]ork always comes next to family, and there is nothing more natural than this."[13] Family orientation is also expressed through the preference for subordinate-superior relationships in the workplace that are analogous to the way that a parent (i.e., the superior) interacts with a child (i.e., the subordinate) and vice versa.

Harmony and Individual Performance Orientation

One of the most vexing issues for leaders steeped in Anglo-style values and practices is establishing reward systems in developing countries that are intended to motivate subordinates to establish and pursue individual goals and objectives. The importance placed on maintaining good and harmonious interpersonal relationships tends to stifle individual performance orientation in developing countries. Subordinates are expected to concentrate on loyalty and compliance toward their superiors and act in ways that promote, rather than disturb, harmony with their co-workers. This means that any action that causes a person to "stand out" within his or her group is frowned upon and may lead to jealousy and isolation of that person. In turn, persons who are having trouble fulfilling their quotas or otherwise keeping up with others will usually be tolerated and treated with compassion as long as they are doing their best and have an honest

---

[13] Id.

intention to contribute to the work of the group.[14] Muczyk and Holt noted that in light of the collectivist nature of many societies classified as "developing" it is not surprising that group and/or organizational measures of performance are recommended as the basis for rewards.[15]

Low Sense of Control and Self-Efficacy

The low levels of sense of control and self-efficacy often found in developing countries cause persons to believe that events are based primarily on external causes outside of their control or influence. As a result, many people in developing countries look at activities such as planning, scheduling, and goal setting as being pointless. They are also reluctant to be proactive and take initiative since they feel that there is little likelihood that such an approach will make a difference, given that results are out of their control, and there are concerns that individual initiative will simply increase risks and uncertainty and that challenging the status quo will disrupt harmony within the group. Poor or mediocre behavior may be explained, and tolerated, in developing countries as simply being a person's "destiny."

Communication Patterns

Aycan noted that organizational communication patterns in developing countries tend to be "indirect, non-assertive, non-confrontational, and usually downwards,"[16] which is consistent with the hierarchical nature of organizations and the acceptance of authority from and at the top of the hierarchy. This has a number of consequences for organizational leaders

---

[14] For further discussion, see Kabasakal, H., and A. Dastmalchian. 2001. "Leadership and Culture in the Middle East." *Applied Psychology: An International Review* 50, no. 4, pp. 559–89.

[15] Muczyk, J.P., and D.T. Holt. May 2008. "Toward a Cultural Contingency Model of Leadership." *Journal of Leadership & Organizational Studies* 14, no. 4, pp. 277–86, 283.

[16] Aycan, Z. 2004. "Leadership and Teamwork in Developing Countries: Challenges and Opportunities." In *Online Readings in Psychology and Culture*, eds. W. Lonner, D. Dinnel, S. Hayes and D. Sattler.

in developing countries. First, honest and complete performance evaluations are extremely difficult since negative feedback, even when intended to improve performance, is seen as when Aycan described as "destructive criticism" and often misconstrued as being a personal attack on the recipient. Feedback, when given, must also be presented in a way that does not cause the recipient to lose "face" among his or her peers and in the eyes of his or her superiors. Finally, negative feedback may be viewed as disrupting the all-important sense of harmony within the group. Second, downward communication patterns mean that little, if any, feedback flows from subordinates up to their superiors. This is not surprising given the deference shown to those in positions of authority; however, the lack of information from lower levels of the organization may undermine the leader's ability to make appropriate decisions and make adjustments to directions that have already been issued. Aycan also noted that "[t]here is strong preference for face-to-face communication in business dealings" in developing countries.[17] While this type of communication should, presumably, reduce the risk of misunderstanding it also tends to be more time-consuming and may lead to delays in completing specific tasks and entire projects.

Leader Authority and Power

The almost absolute authority of superiors in an organizational context in developing countries is consistent with the authority orientation that permeates societal culture in those countries. Superiors are entitled to, and receive, respect, loyalty, and deference and are trusted because of their knowledge, experience, and achievements. While organizational rules may be prescribed, subordinates act based on their respect for authority rather than because they are expected to follow rules and procedures. Subordinates rarely challenge those in authority and accept that while superiors are part of the "in-group" they have a higher status that separates them from other group members and entitles them to certain privileges and advantages. Superiors in developing countries often have close relationships with their subordinates, including close and extensive participation

---

[17] Id.

in the personal lives of subordinates; however, these relationships are not to be confused with "friendship" and typically remain formal and distant.

The respect for, and acceptance of, a leader's authority in developing countries is accompanied by a strong desire among leaders to exercise the power they have been given over their subordinates and their firms. Ideally, at least from the perspective of the subordinates, power will be exercised in a manner that is consistent with good interpersonal relations between leaders and their subordinates—a style that Aycan describes as "benevolent paternalism,"[18] which is characterized by a leader exercising his or her power for the benefit of subordinates in the same way that a parent directs and disciplines his or her children for "their own good." Often, however, leaders in developing countries engage in what Aycan called "exploitative paternalism" and use their power and status for their personal benefit and the advantage of their families and other in-group members.[19] Even when leaders engage in benevolent paternalism they still insist in various manifestations of their power and authority such as formality and respect in personal relationships with subordinates. In addition, the inequality of power between leaders and subordinates leads to centralization and unilateral decision making by the leader. Consultation with subordinates is rare, even nonexistent, since leaders believe that encouraging participation in decision making by subordinates will undermine their power and make them look weak. For their part, subordinates in developing countries are generally tolerant of apparently dictatorial practices of their leaders with respect to decisions and instructions because they trust the wisdom and competencies of the leader and are themselves reluctant to take on the risks and responsibilities that come with making decisions.

Leader Networking Responsibilities

The importance of relationships between leaders and their subordinates in developing countries has already been discussed earlier; however, the relationship orientation typically found in those countries extends

---

[18] Id.

[19] Id.

outside of the workplace in the form of the extensive efforts that leaders in developing countries must make in order to establish and maintain good relations with those in positions of power within key institutions such as the government. The scarcity of technical and financial resources in developing countries, and the role that local politics plays in who controls those resources and how they are allocated, means that organizational leaders in those countries must proactively seek to protect the interests of their firms. Accordingly, Aycan notes that developing countries' leaders must be skilled in "networking and diplomacy."[20]

---

[20] Id.

About the Author

Dr. Alan S. Gutterman is the founding director of the Sustainable Entrepreneurship Project (www.seproject.org). In addition, Alan's prolific output of practical guidance and tools for legal and financial professionals, managers, entrepreneurs, and investors has made him one of the best-selling individual authors in the global legal publishing marketplace. His cornerstone work, *Business Transactions Solution*, is on online-only product available and featured on Thomson Reuters' Westlaw, the world's largest legal content platform, which includes almost 200 book-length modules covering the entire life cycle of a business. Alan has also authored or edited over 70 books on sustainable entrepreneurship, management, business law and transactions, international law business and technology management for a number of publishers including Thomson Reuters, Kluwer, Aspatore, Oxford, Quorum, ABA Press, Aspen, Sweet & Maxwell, Euromoney, Business Expert Press, Harvard Business Publishing, CCH, and BNA. Alan has over three decades of experience as a partner and senior counsel with internationally recognized law firms counseling small and large business enterprises in the areas of general corporate and securities matters, venture capital, mergers and acquisitions, international law and transactions, strategic business alliances, technology transfers and intellectual property, and has also held senior management positions with several technology-based businesses including service as the chief legal officer of a leading international distributor of IT products headquartered in Silicon Valley and as the chief operating officer of an emerging broadband media company. He has been an adjunct faculty member at several colleges and universities, including Boalt Hall, Golden Gate University, Hastings College of Law, Santa Clara University, and the University of San Francisco, teaching classes on a diverse range of topics including corporate finance, venture capital, corporate law, Japanese business law and law and economic development, He received his AB, MBA, and JD from the University of California at Berkeley, a DBA from Golden Gate University, and a PhD from the University of Cambridge. For more information about Alan and his activities, please contact him directly at alangutterman@gmail.com, follow him on LinkedIn (https://www.linkedin.com/in/alangutterman/) and visit his website at alangutterman.com, which includes an extensive collection of links to his books and other publications and resource materials for students and practitioners of sustainable entrepreneurship.

Index

OTHER TITLES IN THE HUMAN RESOURCE MANAGEMENT AND ORGANIZATIONAL BEHAVIOR COLLECTION

- *Conflict First Aid: How to Stop Personality Clashes and Disputes from Damaging You or Your Organization* by Nancy Radford
- *How to Manage Your Career: The Power of Mindset in Fostering Success* by Kelly Swingler
- *Deconstructing Management Maxims, Volume I: A Critical Examination of Conventional Business Wisdom* by Kevin Wayne
- *Deconstructing Management Maxims, Volume II: A Critical Examination of Conventional Business Wisdom* by Kevin Wayne
- *The Real Me: Find and Express Your Authentic Self* by Mark Eyre
- *Across the Spectrum: What Color Are You?* by Stephen Elkins-Jarrett
- *The Human Resource Professional's Guide to Change Management: Practical Tools and Techniques to Enact Meaningful and Lasting Organizational Change* by Melanie J. Peacock
- *Tough Calls: How to Move Beyond Indecision and Good Intentions* by Linda D. Henman
- *The 360 Degree CEO: Generating Profits While Leading and Living with Passion and Principles* by Lorraine A. Moore
- *The Concise Coaching Handbook: How to Coach Yourself and Others to Get Business Results* by Elizabeth Dickinson

Announcing the Business Expert Press Digital Library

Concise e-books business students need for classroom and research

This book can also be purchased in an e-book collection by your library as

- a one-time purchase,
- that is owned forever,
- allows for simultaneous readers,
- has no restrictions on printing, and
- can be downloaded as PDFs from within the library community.

Our digital library collections are a great solution to beat the rising cost of textbooks. E-books can be loaded into their course management systems or onto students' e-book readers.
The **Business Expert Press** digital libraries are very affordable, with no obligation to buy in future years. For more information, please visit **www.businessexpertpress.com/librarians**. To set up a trial in the United States, please email **sales@businessexpertpress.com**.